Shattered Vows

Debra Laaser

Shattered Vows

Hope and Healing

for Women

Who Have Been

Sexually Betrayed

ZONDERVAN®

ZONDERVAN.com/
AUTHORTRACKER
follow your favorite authors

Shattered Vows
Copyright © 2008 by Debra Laaser

Requests for information should be addressed to:

Zondervan, *Grand Rapids, Michigan* 49530

Library of Congress Cataloging-in-Publication Data

Laaser, Debra.
    Shattered vows : hope and healing for women who have been sexually
betrayed / Debra Laaser.
        p.   cm.
    Includes bibliographical references.
    ISBN-13: 978-0-310-27394-3
    ISBN-10: 0-310-27394-3
    1. Adultery. 2. Wives — Psychology. 3. Marriage. 4. Marriage — Religious
aspects — Christianity. I. Title.
HQ806.L28   2008
248.8'435 — dc22   2007026419

Interior design by Beth Shagene

Printed in the United States of America

08 09 10 11 12 13 • 22 21 20 19 18 17 16 15 14 13 12 11 10 9 8 7 6 5 4 3 2 1

To my twin sister, Barbara Mauro,
who lost her battle with colon cancer
as I was in the final stages of editing this book.

Contents

Acknowledgments

If someone had told me twenty years ago that the adversity in my life would one day birth a book about sexual betrayal, I would have said they were crazy. Despite my best efforts to remain in the shadows of folks who have more formal training, God seemed to keep seeking me out through some very special people to write a book that would serve hurting women.

I wish to thank Jennifer Cisney, a friend and colleague at the American Association of Christian Counselors who created the first safe platform for me to tell my story publicly. With her gentle encouragement and interview skills, she walked me into the world of videotaping that began my "coming out." By reviewing reels of videotapes that she had collected of our work together, she penned the beginning of my story so I could get started. Jennifer has been a cheerleader of my journey for years and the impetus for my writing.

I have a deep appreciation and love for my best friend and twenty-year business partner, Mary Munger. She was the first one "on the scene" when my life appeared shattered from sexual betrayal. And she has lived through more of my thoughts, feelings, highlights, and lowlights than anyone else I know. She is an angel in disguise with bits of wisdom that flow in every conversation. I remember when I first told her I would be writing this book, I said, "I'm really afraid to go back and relive all of those shattered years." She wisely responded, "Deb, I'm sure it will be difficult, but at least this time you will know the outcome." Her gifts surround my writing space to remind me of what I can do. Thank you, Mary, for being such a devoted friend.

I have also been blessed by Johna Hale—a spiritual mentor and friend who led me through the difficult transition from my secular career to my ministry with women. She also held me up in prayer through the emotional process of writing and kept me focused on God's desire that I share my experience, strength, and hope with other women.

Elizabeth Griffin agreed to join me in 2001 to cofacilitate process groups for women at our center for healing. With her twenty-five years of experience working in the field of sexual offending and addiction and my personal experience as a recovering wife of an addict, we became a dynamic team to serve women. Elizabeth has been a teacher, supporter, and friend, and to her credit, I have grown immensely as we have worked together. Many of my insights for this book developed as we taught and led our women's groups.

I am reminded of the great love of both my parents and Mark's parents as I write. From both of their marriages, I witnessed "staying" and persevering. I know that their mentoring of long marriages is what kept me "figuring it out" rather than running away in those early months of pain. My parents have celebrated over sixty years of marriage, and I so appreciate all that they have done to sustain a committed relationship and to demonstrate that a family is worth fighting for.

I would not be here writing as a transformed woman had it not been for the years of therapy with Maureen Graves. She is the most gifted therapist I have ever known. And I am quite sure that Mark and I were led by God to Maureen and Tom Graves as part of his master plan for our lives. There are no words to describe my gratitude for the presence and gentleness that Maureen brought to my healing. She knows every nook and cranny of my soul! If there is ever a woman I seek to emulate, it would be Maureen.

I feel privileged to have Sandy Vander Zicht as my editor. Sandy approached me many years ago—I think it was actually ten!—and encouraged me to write a book for women. Several times we talked, she prayed over me and patiently waited for God's timing. When I accepted God's "nudge" to be a spokesperson for hurting women, Sandy assured me that I was the right woman to write this book. Having Sandy believe in me when it was hard to believe in myself was a great gift.

My collaborative writer, Traci Mullins, became the "wind beneath my wings." Introduced to me by Sandy Vander Zicht, Traci was my companion, friend, editorial expert, and writing therapist! With wit and patience, she coached me to find my writing rhythm and confidence in my writing abilities. She walked with me hand in hand to birth my first book—and a birthing process it was! I will be forever indebted to Traci for her professional gifts as a writer as well as her personal gifts as a friend.

I have a full heart as I think of many others who have supported me as a person and encouraged my writing, speaking, and support of women: Patrick Carnes, Jennifer Schneider, Mike and Linda Richards, Tim Clinton, Daniel Amen, Carol and Darv Smith, Heidi Brizendine, Eli Machen, and Dave Carder are just a few. I am thankful for the hundreds of women and couples who have shared the most intimate details and struggles of their lives with me during my years of being a "hope bearer" for them. Their stories have clarified my wisdom about the healing journey from sexual betrayal and reminded me of God's faithfulness to transform us if we are willing to be led through the pain.

Although my twin sister, Barb, was never officially engaged in a recovery program, she was a constant reminder to me of the desire of so many people to improve relationships. Barb had a heart for understanding the stories behind the people she knew and loved. She was one of my grandest supporters and will be a part of me in ways I cannot describe—a twin connection. I miss you dearly, Barb.

My three children, Sarah, Jonathan, and Benjamin, truly light up my life. Their precious faces kept me going when I had no desire to go on twenty years ago. I thank you Sarah, Jon, and Ben for your genuine interest in and encouragement of my writing project this past year. I am so blessed by you and the loving hearts you have today.

I wear my thirty-year anniversary ring with great pride, for it symbolizes the reward of great dedication to a healing journey. I am so proud of Mark and what he has done with his life. My destination would have been very different if he had not taken his behaviors seriously and been willing to seek change. He is one who has truly been broken by his betrayal and has sought God's guidance and redemption ever since. I consider it an honor to come alongside a man who seeks to serve God with all of his heart in his "second chance." Thank you, Mark, for being a faith-filled servant and a devoted husband.

There is no doubt in my mind that God has empowered my fingers to type the thousands of words that fill this book. I know that it has been his desire to use my story to bring hope to his people. I am embarrassed to admit how I have fought the process. I have doubted my abilities. I have been stuck without resolve and have "given up" too many times to count. And yet time and time again, as I turned this project over to him each writing day, words and stories began to flow. Thank you, Lord, for your faithfulness in my journey and in this book. May readers be blessed by the pages that follow ...

The Darkest, Loneliest Day

L ast summer our local television station broadcast the devastation of a tornado that wiped out an entire farm in our state of Minnesota—fourteen buildings in all. No adults were home at the time—just three teenage siblings. The kids hid under the staircase in the basement and literally watched their house blow off its foundation and vanish right before their eyes. They reported that the loud winds and pounding rain lasted about three minutes. And then it was totally calm. No sounds. No rain. Nothing but debris, everywhere.

My heart ached—for the family for sure. But it also ached from the memory of the tornado that had swept away my "house" almost twenty years before. One moment I was living the life I had always wanted. In high school I fell in love with and later married the man of my dreams. At thirty-seven, I had been married for fifteen years and had three beautiful children. My husband was a successful and respected pastoral counselor in our midwestern town. I had just started my own business with my best friend. Life was good. I never imagined that the roof and walls could blow off my life in just a few minutes. But just as that tornado blew away everything but the people in three short minutes, so in about the same amount of time, the winds carrying the lies and deception in my marriage blew away everything for me.

On an otherwise normal morning in March, my world came to a crashing halt when my husband, Mark, came home from work with two of his colleagues—the marriage and family therapist and the medical doctor who worked at the health center where Mark was a pastoral counselor. They asked me to join them in the living room because they had something to tell me. I scurried around asking my business partner to take our youngest child with her—the other two were in school. There was a sense of urgency and heaviness in the somberness of the visitors who invited themselves into my home. I was irritated that they hadn't at least called to say they were coming. I was thinking it was rude to expect that I would be ready for company with no notice. My mind was scrambling, trying to fill the ominous silence with *something*. They took their chairs while Mark slumped down in our navy blue wing chair. I remember thinking how pale he looked. No one was smiling or making small talk. I restlessly took a seat on the couch.

Within the next few minutes, I was told that Mark had been living a secret life. They said he had been sexually inappropriate with some of his clients and that he had lied to the staff and to me. They informed me of all of the ways he had broken his wedding vows and even called him a sexual pervert. They were cool, proper, and unwavering as they announced that they had fired Mark from his job. After the several sentences of explanation, they asked me if I had any questions. That was all—did I have any questions?

Of course I had questions! Are you people idiots? Are you sure you have the right guy? You can't be describing *my* husband. He wouldn't do things like that. I know—we've been intimate partners for fifteen years. He loves me and loves our kids. He would never do anything like that. Are you crazy, thinking you can march into my house and in a matter of five minutes expose these awful secrets and then fire my husband? How do you think we'll live? What do you expect me to do? Where is your compassion? Is the situation really so bad? How can you be so calm if you are true friends and colleagues? Why do you just sit there so properly? *Why don't you defend him and help us?*

But I said, "No, I don't have any questions." And they left—just like that. Five minutes was all it took to deconstruct my whole reality.

Feeling stunned and disoriented, yet strangely calm, I lifted my head to glance at Mark. He was slouched in the corner of the chair, expressionless and motionless, with tears rolling down his face. I know it was only God who nudged me off the couch to go to him and put my arms around him and just weep. Neither of us spoke for a long time, but I heard whispers that must have been from God: "There are missing pieces in your life together—trust me to lead you to a richer place." I had an inexplicable sense that God was somehow at work in my life, even in this dreadfully dark and lonely hour.

This book is about the hope that existed even in those darkest moments and grew deep and sustaining over time as I made critical choices that would ultimately bring about a healing I couldn't have imagined. If you have been sexually betrayed by your husband, you are likely to question whether you will ever feel love in your marriage again. As you grieve the loss of what you thought you had, I want you to know that it is possible to experience transformation in your life—and even in your marriage. As you read my story and many others, I hope that you, too, will find hope and healing.

So Much for "Happily Ever After"

Every woman who has been sexually betrayed recalls with vivid clarity that darkest, loneliest day when betrayal entered the sanctuary of her marriage and forever changed her life. The marriage she thought was built on truth and trust was laced with lies and deceit. She wonders how she will ever deal with the pain she is experiencing.

What exactly is the sexual betrayal that wounds so deeply? A husband's infidelity may consist of many different components—sexual fantasy, pornography, masturbation, cybersex, Internet chat rooms, massage parlors, strip clubs, emotional or physical affairs, and prostitutes. Here is the problem a wife faces: her husband has been unfaithful to their marriage vows. He has lusted after, inappropriately touched, or been sexual with another person—sometimes several people. And no matter how the horrific information came to light, she feels terribly alone. Listen to the experiences of some other women whose stories might be different from yours but whose hearts ache in similar ways.

Candace

It was an ordinary day of packing lunches for the kids, running errands, and making a few calls for my home-based business. I was taking my husband's clothes to the cleaners when a crumpled piece of paper fell out of his pocket displaying numerous names of women. I could feel my face flush and my pulse race as nausea swept over me. I could barely give the clerk the information for the dry cleaning order. I walked numbly to my car, collapsed in the driver's seat, and began shaking all over. Panic engulfed me. I couldn't think what to do next. "Breathe ... breathe ..." was the only thought I could hold on to.

I accomplished nothing that day; mostly I just stared into space. I confronted Jeff that night, and he denied knowing anything about those names. In fact, he had no idea how that paper could have even gotten into his pocket! My anxiety would not cease, and in fact, terror overcame me the next day. Tears kept flowing, anger was growing, but I had no information to support my reaction. I was privately planning my detective work to uncover facts about those names. My brain was locked on thoughts of finding out the truth.

Later the second night, Jeff confessed that he had been seeing a woman while on a business trip. It was "no big deal," he said, "just some drinks and socializing." I found myself doubting his confession. I couldn't help the rage that was overtaking me — and the obsession with those women's names. I felt as if I were going mad. After I spent another week crying, blaming Jeff, and distancing myself from him, he admitted that my intuition was right: he had had several affairs — some one-night stands, some longer lasting.

I'd finally gotten the truth I'd wanted, but I actually felt worse rather than better. I'd always thought I could handle anything; I was independent, resourceful, a leader. But that day, I had no idea what to do. I collapsed in a heap until I could choke out a call to my pastor.

Paula

I always suspected that Jerry was up to something when he stayed up late at night, making excuses for not coming to bed with me. I could barely stay awake to watch the news, and I hated that we didn't go to bed at the same time. I felt I was disappointing him because I had no energy to talk or be sexual after a long day with our three small children.

One night when I couldn't sleep, I got up and walked into the living room. I found Jerry there masturbating while watching pornography on his computer. I was shocked and had a lot of questions. He quickly shut down his computer and said tonight was the first time anything like this had happened—really. He was sorry; he would never do it again. He looked sincere, and I wanted to believe him. I slipped back under the covers trembling with anger and sadness.

Only a few weeks later I caught him again. I knew he wouldn't want me to be upset with him, and I hoped that if I didn't make a big deal out of the behavior, he would stop doing it. I couldn't imagine telling anyone about this; it was embarrassing and seemed so out of character for my husband. But deep inside I felt exceedingly ashamed and frightened about what was wrong with us.

Delores

I have found myself pulling away from my husband more and more because it seems as though he is constantly watching other women. I feel so hurt and inadequate around him; there must be something wrong with me. I know I've gained some weight since the children were born. Still, I don't like it one bit when we go to restaurants or church and he is constantly gazing at women or trying to strike up conversations with them. When I've asked him about it, he says I'm just insecure and I need to get over it. I don't know what else I can do.

Denisha

My husband, Jerome, recently attended his fifteen-year high school reunion and has been emailing an old "friend" constantly since then. When I asked him about this friend, he said she was just a girl he used to date in high school. They hadn't talked since they had graduated and both left for college. It is now several months later, and I've noticed that she has sent pictures and small gifts to him and often calls him now, too. I feel uncomfortable with the situation, but Jerome tells me nothing is going on and I shouldn't be so paranoid and jealous.

Rita

Nico was acting so strange one day that I finally asked him what was going on. He said he couldn't live with himself any longer if he didn't confess something to me. He had been having an affair with someone I knew. The "someone" happened to be one of my best friends. I don't think I have ever felt so much rage. When all of the truth was exposed, I was faced with the reality that he had actually slept with *three* of my friends and had seen prostitutes as well. I began to wonder if my headaches in the past year were related to what Nico had finally disclosed.

Patty

My husband and I are best friends. We tell each other everything — except for all of the secrets he has been hiding about looking at neighborhood women through their windows. I always thought he was just going out for a walk. One night, a police officer brought him home after catching him window peeping a few houses away. My life was turned upside down.

Danika

Kristoffer is my second husband, and he has been consistently attentive to me on every level these past three years. I have never felt so cared about and cherished by a man. I have trusted him completely with my heart. Even after living through the pain of divorce, I never could have imagined the agony that would accompany discovering that my new husband had become emotionally involved with another woman. Kristoffer says that he loves me deeply and hasn't had any physical contact with the woman. He says they have only been seeing each other at restaurants and emailing each other. I want to believe him, but how can I ever feel cherished by him the way I did? He is clearly torn in half by his feelings for someone else. How could he have let this happen? What are we supposed to do now?

Kim

Over the thirteen years we have been married, my husband has traveled monthly for business. I had no idea he had been posting his profile on the Internet to connect with women in the towns he was visiting. One of my neighbors saw his ad and called me. At first he told me he was just experimenting with the process—he had no intention of actually meeting anyone. But after one of his "connections" found out he was married, she called me to let me know what he was doing. When he was caught, he decided to file for divorce. I was left alone with our four little girls, and as a stay-at-home mom, I feel totally stuck. He has ruined my life.

Simone

My husband was fired from his executive position after being caught using pornography on his company's network computer. I work for the same organization, so the situation is extremely awkward for me. Without his salary, I can't really leave my job, but I feel so much shame knowing that everyone at work is aware of our situation. I have difficulty even getting out of bed in the morning.

Secrets and Signs

Women all over the world are living with these kinds of heartaches, yet women who are affected by sexual betrayal often feel that no one else could possibly know what they are going through.

When Mark's story, which included sexual contact with several of the women he had counseled, became front-page news in our local paper, I thought I must be the only wife who had ever lived through this nightmare. "Just give us our scarlet *A*'s and let the world sneer and judge," I thought bitterly. I had no choice but to let the world in on my secret. I felt humiliated, ashamed, and marked for life. I couldn't imagine anyone accepting us. It may seem strange to some that I felt all of these things—after all, it was Mark's behavior that was being reported! I later learned about the "couple shame" that almost always accompanies sexual sin in a marriage.

Many commonalities exist between my story and the ones I hear every day in my work with women who have been devastated by their husbands' infidelity. Although I had been married for fifteen years and had dated Mark for four years before we married, the disclosure of his sexual behavior still came as a total surprise to me. I had no idea he was living a double life—a beloved husband, father, pastor, and counselor, as well as a deceitful, secretive, lustful, and lonely man. I thought I knew him. I thought he shared everything with me. How could I have been so blind? While some people would judge Mark harshly for his lying during all those years, my primary feeling was "How could *I* have been so stupid and naive?" I had missed all of the signs. I thought I was an intelligent person, a "good wife." How could I have been completely clueless about a major part of my husband's life?

Other women have noticed signs of potentially problematic sexual behaviors even before they committed to marriage. Some found X-rated movies in their boyfriend's home or witnessed him surfing for pornographic images on his computer. Some were aware that their loved one had accompanied friends to strip clubs or massage parlors for a "guys' night out." Many women felt pressure to be sexual early in the relationship. Some knew their partner had been sexual with many others before them. Some knew that it was an affair that began their own relationship with their current spouse. Often they noticed that the man who said he only had eyes for them had roaming eyes for many other women, perhaps even hugging or touching other women far more than seemed appropriate. In almost all cases, these women thought the behavior would stop as soon as they were married, so they disregarded the signs that something might be wrong.

Even when the signs are clear, women have differing reactions. For example, when Anika caught her new husband in an affair, she confronted him and insisted they go to therapy. After they spent several months "working it out," she assumed the problem was resolved, and they never talked about it again. Vanessa knew about her husband's use of pornography well before she agreed to marry him. When it continued after their wedding, she decided it wasn't that bad because she thought every man needed an outlet for his sexual drive. She couldn't keep up with his desire for sex, and in a way it was a relief to her to know he could "take care of it." Frances was a Christian missionary and a devoted wife. Although her husband couldn't seem to stop engaging with prostitutes, she believed she was called to love him and stand by him no matter what. And Lorena decided that the best way to handle her husband's excessive desire for "passion" was to join him by participating in sex games with which she felt totally uncomfortable.

When we have new information about sexual betrayal in our marriage, most of us tend to revisit our past in an effort to recognize signs of behaviors that were unacceptable, uncomfortable, or undesired in our relationship. We all had ways of dealing with those signs: some we ignored, some we resented, some we joined in on, and some we minimized or denied. As we seek to heal, we will learn to listen to our wisdom about signs we see and to respond in ways that are congruent with how we feel and what we need. It is a process that takes time.

You Are Not Alone

Regardless of how you found out about sexual betrayal in your relationship, how long you have known about it, and what you have chosen to do with the information, you are not alone. Women have struggled silently and shamefully, trying to figure out how to deal with this sensitive, heartbreaking information. It is terribly confusing to experience life with your husband as "normal" in so many ways—to feel like best friends, spend a lot of time together, raise happy children, succeed in careers—and then be crushed by the behaviors of a straying spouse.

Tarah, an intelligent, extroverted wife, said to me during our first visit, "This may sound bizarre, but I think it's easier for someone to have heard about a cancer diagnosis than this because at least they can talk about it with other people and get their support. I can't talk at all because people would only judge—they wouldn't understand."

Many questions fill your mind after the disclosure: How could this have happened? How could I love him again? Will I ever be able to trust him again? Why would I want to stay? Will I ever feel like letting him touch me again? Should I sleep with him? Should I make him move out? Will my pain ever go away? Is there really any hope that our lives could be the way they were? Will I ever have back the man I thought I married?

When sexual infidelity of any kind shatters your dreams of feeling chosen and cherished forever, your emotions take you on a sickening roller-coaster ride: I love him. I hate him. I want him out! I can't stand to think of living without him. This can't be true. It can't be happening to me. This has to be a bad dream. My friends tell me to leave. My kids tell me to stay. My pastor tells me to try to be a better wife. My world is crashing down and there is nothing I can do. Everything I thought I had is over. God surely will save my marriage. I must be patient. I can't stand this chaos another minute. I can't seem to do anything. I will not let this destroy me. Can there be meaning in my suffering? Maybe God hasn't abandoned us. Maybe there is something more ...

There *is* something more. It is possible to grow through and even heal from sexual betrayal. You don't have to stay stuck with your swirling thoughts of indecision, loneliness, rage, shame, and hopelessness. You don't need to be a victim, seemingly ruined and without choices. And you certainly don't need to be alone.

If your "happily ever after" dreams lay smashed at your feet, then I invite you to come with me on a journey toward hope and transformation. This is not a path for the fainthearted. It takes great courage, endurance, and patience. But your story of shattered vows does not have to end here. In the pages ahead, you will be given the tools and opportunity to learn about yourself in ways that will empower you to make decisions that are right for you.

During the past several years, I have cofacilitated wives' therapy groups and, through their stories, have broadened my understanding of betrayed women. Each of the nine chapters in this book is based on my own experience and theirs.

1. *What Am I Supposed to Do Now?* When a woman is betrayed sexually, she has many specific questions about what to do. She will be guided to trust her feelings, seeking out wisdom, and listening to promptings from God to take the next right steps.

2. *Why Should I Get Help When It's His Problem?* The greatest enemy of any problem is isolation. Participating in safe community is essential to getting the support and healing you need after betrayal. When a husband and wife share an emotional and spiritual life together, sexual intimacy becomes a healthy expression of that connectedness. When a couple's connection is unhealthy, however—or when betrayal tragically breaks it—then they have an opportunity to heal their deepest problem, which is an intimacy disorder.

3. *How Could This Have Happened?* Understanding what is going on beneath the devastation of sexual betrayal can be very helpful. The behaviors that have been so hurtful are only a small part of what is really felt, believed, and desired. Healing requires an understanding of the deeper issues.

4. *Where Can I Hide My Heart?* A woman who has been betrayed experiences many practical and emotional losses. Faced with the reality of these losses, she needs to find ways to protect herself from sadness, anger, loneliness, and anxiety. Grieving loss is an important part of healing, as is finding purpose in her pain and loss.

5. *When Will I Stop Feeling So Out of Control?* A woman is powerless over her reactions, her emotions, and her husband and his behaviors. The acceptance of powerlessness can lead to brokenness and surrender, humility and empathy. If both husband and wife reach this place, they can begin to be intimate companions on the journey toward healing. If a woman's husband hasn't chosen to accept his need for grace, her acceptance of it for herself will free her from anger, bitterness, fruitless efforts to control, and a victim mentality.

6. *What Do You Mean, "Do I Want to Get Well"?* This chapter poses a question that every betrayed wife must answer for herself: To what lengths am I willing to go to heal myself and my marriage? Understanding what is beneath betrayal will take time and commitment. It can lead to a journey of self-examination and change for richer relationships in all of life.

7. *How Can I Ever Trust Him Again?* Rebuilding trust is a process that takes time. Sometimes a wife believes that if her spouse would live "perfectly," then she could trust him again. As part of the process, she will learn how to trust the intent of his heart. She'll also learn how important it is to trust herself and to trust God.

8. *Is Forgiving Him Really Possible?* Forgiveness is another process that requires patience. Forgiving an unfaithful spouse is healthy and biblical, but many roadblocks can halt the process. Forgiveness that is offered too quickly can actually undermine lasting healing. When a woman works at forgiving authentically, she will see a change in her behaviors and in her attitude toward her spouse. She'll also feel freedom from being a victim of his behaviors.

9. *How Can We Rebuild Our Relationship?* This chapter offers resounding hope and practical guidance to couples seeking the deepest level of healing for their broken relationship. Getting on the same page — perhaps for the first time — and forging a powerful new alliance in the aftermath of shattered vows is a dream within reach. Creativity and passion begin to flow as couples learn to be true companions and to work as a team, each bringing strengths to the overall vision of the ways in which God will bless their marriage.

In many ways, I'm no different than you as you begin this journey of discovery and healing; I'm just a few more years down the road of recovery. I'm still trying to know God more intimately and depend on him more completely. I still react to certain situations as if the painful past were repeating itself, even when it isn't. I still cope badly sometimes and damage my relationships. I can still feel inadequate, afraid, left out, unchosen, and lost. I can still be irritable, impatient, and desperate for others to take care of me. What is so different for me today is that I know myself so much better — what I feel, why I react, what I need, and who to go to for help. And it takes me much less time to maneuver through an uncomfortable situation or change unhealthy behaviors. The fruits of God's Spirit — love, joy, peace, patience, kindness, gentleness, goodness, faithfulness, and self-control — are definitely more a part of my life now than they were twenty years ago. I choose not to be alone when I am in pain. I live much more spontaneously, enjoying the moments of each day. I have greater understanding, acceptance, empathy, trust, and ability to surrender—and more unconditional love for myself and others. Perhaps most important, I know I have choices—always.

Although my story and the stories of others in this book will deal with the specifics of surviving and living beyond sexual betrayal, for me this journey continues to be far more about *growing up spiritually* through sexual betrayal. Everything about this adversity has invited me to take steps toward experiencing a deeper dependence on God and others. I had really never experienced being totally honest with anyone except my husband. I didn't know how to let other people deep into my life, to be authentic from the core of my being. Little did I know I was about to be pulled far outside my comfort zone—challenged to choose healing and wholeness through sharing my hurts, feelings, doubts, fears, and weaknesses with other safe people. God would use true Christian fellowship to speak truth into me—to grow me spiritually.

As you read this book, my prayer for you is that you, too, will experience the gift of spiritual growth as a result of living through the devastation of shattered vows. I know such an idea may not sound conceivable—or even desirable!—in this moment. But adversity can lead us to do extraordinary things and to seek greatness for our character and our relationships. As you learn to lean on God for each step of your journey, I hope you will discover much more of the woman you are meant to be and a life that is more joyful, purpose-filled, and authentic.

CHAPTER 1

What Am I Supposed to Do Now?

First Steps for the Brokenhearted

Perseverance is more prevailing than adversity, and many things which cannot be overcome when they are together, yield themselves up when taken little by little.

Adapted from Plutarch (46–120 AD), *Lives*

"Consider the ravens: They do not sow or reap, they have no storeroom or barn; yet God feeds them. And how much more valuable you are than birds!"

Luke 12:24

When I first met Mark, I was seventeen. Although I had plans to go to college, I became more interested in what he was going to do and what dreams he was pursuing. They were magnificent. Mark was a debater, a college tennis player, an academic award winner—with plans to go to seminary and be a pastor. Wow! I did continue with my plans to go to college, but my focus was on hurrying through so that I could be married to the man of my dreams. All the while Mark and I attended separate colleges, my heart was miles away, dreaming of the day when I would immerse myself in my husband's life. I was already making sacrifices of things I wanted to do in order to be with him. I had no idea that I was starting down a path of silent resentment and sadness with no healthy way to talk about it.

I was in shock after the living room conference in which I was briefed of Mark's secret behavior. Mark's first steps were made for him very quickly during the intervention his colleagues held before delivering the news to me. First, they fired him from all of his work. Second, they advised him to get deep and comprehensive psychological and spiritual help for his "symptoms" of acting out sexually in such destructive ways.

One of the men who participated in confronting Mark was a recovering alcoholic. I soon learned that this colleague had told my husband that his problems seemed similar to his own, and he offered to find help for Mark. Within three days Mark left for a thirty-day inpatient treatment program for sexual addiction. It was a whirlwind of phone conversations, intake interviews, and packing. Our lives were in emergency mode, with all sirens blasting. My husband went off to get help, leaving me at home with three small children and no income in the foreseeable future.

Life was not looking good for me. Mark at least was being rescued from despair and furnished with a plan. But no one talked to *me* about first steps. What should *I* be doing? Could anyone out there advise me on how to handle my emotions, my bills, my choices, or my marriage? Even though the story of what Mark had done was front-page news in our local paper, no one from our church or social circles reached out to me. I felt totally alone.

I quickly took on the persona I had adopted at other times during my life when storms of any kind hit: I tried to look perfectly calm. I could barely think or feel, let alone decide practical things to do, so I went into autopilot mode, which for me meant "getting busy doing something." I determined that we would get through this. I didn't have an urge to run away because, practically, that wasn't a great option for me. I had three kids, and my family was five hundred miles away. Besides, it was not what I knew—I had parents who had modeled commitment and were still together after forty-two years of marriage. They had never talked about leaving each other.

I suppose I could have considered going to someone for help or advice, but the thought didn't even cross my mind. Figuring out difficult situations by myself was what I knew how to do. It was far too embarrassing to expose more information or need to someone else. I did what I do best: I kept my feelings to myself and worked ceaselessly at figuring out how to manage my life. It kept me busy and distracted me from thinking about the devastation. I was grateful for necessary things to focus on so that my crying didn't consume my entire day.

After Mark left for the inpatient treatment program, I was flooded with practical dilemmas: What do I tell the kids? Who else should I tell? How will I take care of our bills? Have I been exposed to sexually transmitted diseases? How can I focus on my work and the kids' needs when I'm such a mess inside? Will I ever stop crying? Do I really know everything that happened? Can there be more? How can I prevent this from happening again? Are the children safe? Am I crazy thinking we can overcome this? Am I just being naive thinking I can trust again? Do couples really "make it" after something like this?

I was good at being a martyr, and for now, it was serving me well. I would just figure out how to do it all! First things first for me involved thinking about how to shore up our finances. Previously Mark had handled all of our money, and I needed to sort through the bills to pay. I was devastated to find months and months of unopened bank statements and overdue invoices. I could see that the details of managing our home had been abandoned, and I was terrified. Furthermore, it was nearing time to pay taxes. We owed several thousand dollars but had no resources to pay the IRS. And now I was alone to figure out what we were going to do. The compassion and patience I had felt in the first few days after Mark agreed to get help were giving way to frustration and rage. It was one thing for him to violate our sacred marriage vows, but now I was feeling abandoned and uncared for in another way. The kids and I were unsafe financially, and I hadn't even realized it.

I can move very fast when I'm not feeling safe! Action to figure out how to survive pulled me right out of much of my sadness; I was busy doing the next thing in front of me. I decided to escalate the growth of my newly created company so that somehow it would support us. My business partner and I worked out a plan to allow me to work longer hours and travel more. I traveled forty-three out of fifty-two weekends the following year, selling our artwork at various art shows throughout the Midwest. Working gave me a sense of being in control—at least of my own destiny—and of knowing that I could take care of myself and my children if I needed to. Work was my friend; it was comforting; it was a place I could leave behind my anxieties and confusion about the rest of my life.

Shortly after Mark left for treatment, his parents called to ask if they could help me in any way. They asked if I needed money. I wanted to say no, that we were fine. But my fear trumped my practiced response. "Yes," I said meekly. "I don't know how I will take care of our taxes." I agreed to accept the financial help that Mark's parents offered, even though it nearly killed me to have to do so. They sent a check to cover all of our taxes—no questions asked.

I found that mixed feelings accompanied almost everything that happened in those first weeks and months. While I was relieved to know we wouldn't be in trouble with the government, I was extremely ashamed to have to admit we were so destitute. I told myself that good, hardworking people should manage money successfully. I believed something must be wrong with us if we had to accept handouts.

Only a week after one of our neighbors read the account of Mark's "fall" in the newspaper, he came over and handed me two hundred dollars. He said he knew things must be difficult for me and that he and his wife wanted to help. Would I please accept his gift? Through tearful eyes, I thanked him for caring and told him the money would be very helpful. When the door closed, my uncontrollable tears were evidence of how much I needed to feel seen and heard. My neighbor's gesture comforted me. "Maybe someone out there does know how hard this is for me," I thought.

Getting Support

Fortunately, treatment centers invite spouses and family members to participate in "Family Week"—a time of education, counseling, and controlled interaction with the patient. The third week of Mark's treatment, I left for my five-hour drive to the treatment center. The fear of meeting with therapists and being an emotional wreck and wondering what was going to happen to us felt almost paralyzing to me. I had never driven that far (five hours) by myself, and I was very concerned about even getting myself there.

But Family Week proved to be a powerful week of connecting with Mark in new, vulnerable conversation. We shared pain and stories of the past; we learned from therapists and educators; we met other men and women who were struggling to heal from sexual betrayal. I was astonished to find myself feeling more alive and authentic in my relationship with Mark than ever before. It felt like a new beginning for us. It was also the beginning for me of experiencing *safe community.* I was very grateful these first steps were available. I shudder to think how our recovery would have been affected if I had been left to fend for myself that entire month.

Some women have taken a first step to get direction or support from a friend, pastor, or therapist, and have been given information that simply stopped their efforts: "Just be a better wife, and these problems won't keep happening," suggests one pastor. "Your husband is totally selfish and will never change," offers an indignant sister to an angry and confused wife. "You would be better off leaving him and finding a man who will love you the way you deserve." A concerned friend says, "I would never stay with my husband if he did those things." The advice keeps pouring in from people trying to help, and it only serves to perplex and paralyze your hurting heart.

I know how difficult it is to find motivation to take first steps after a life-altering tragedy—of any kind. You are already flooded with feelings prompted by painful information. You have important practical things to attend to, but no energy to do anything. You may be getting too much advice or too little help to know how to move on. But only you can take your first steps on a healing journey, and they need to be *for you*. If you are facing a relationship damaged by sexual betrayal, nothing is more important right now than getting help for yourself. You are worth it! If you have children, getting help for yourself is the best thing you can do for them as well. If you are like I was, you are doing a lot of crying alone. You are obsessing about how this could have happened to you. You are replaying your life and wondering where you went wrong. You are beginning to feel crazy and out of control—alone. You need and deserve companionship now.

While you may have thought your mom, sister, or best friend would be the safe person you could talk to, that's not always the case. Often our friends and relatives are so invested in trying to keep us from being in pain that they can do little but try to fix our problems or give advice. It is very difficult to watch a daughter or sister or close friend suffer, and the natural inclination is to get them out of the troubling situation. Finding solutions or explanations is the easiest way, and so you may be bombarded by people trying to get you to a happier place. Unfortunately, these attempts don't always work, or if they do, they are only a Band-Aid that soon wears off. The truly safe people you need now have experienced betrayal and have been counseled in healing. They know how to listen, they aren't afraid of feelings, they don't judge, and they participate in being vulnerable and sharing their struggles, too. You'll discover they are real companions, not just observers or fixers.

We'll talk much more about getting help and participating in safe community in the next chapter. Meanwhile, I know you have many practical questions. I get phone calls and emails almost daily from wives who want to know what to do. Some say they don't even know how to get through the day; others wonder what they can do differently to keep their husbands from acting out again. Many wives are confused about who to talk to; most don't know whether to leave, make him leave, or stay together in the house even though the walls have come tumbling down. Women want solutions—specific solutions—and guarantees. I think all of us would like to believe that if we do the right things, then we can regain confidence that our lives can be the same again—or at the very least, a lot better than they are right now.

There are no black-and-white answers to any of these questions. There are no right answers or wrong answers regarding how to respond to information about infidelity. All women have different experiences, different reactions, different needs, and different solutions. I want to encourage you to take what fits and leave what doesn't. That wisdom comes from the powerful 12-step programs that have led many people up from the lowest bottoms of devastation. Only you will know what is right for you, so you will need to get in touch with your feelings, your body, your intuition, and God; this book will help you do that. Your discoveries will lead you to the next best step God has in mind for *you.* "'For I know the plans I have for you,' declares the LORD, 'plans to prosper you and not to harm you, plans to give you hope and a future'" (Jer. 29:11). I was amazed to feel the hope that returned to me whenever I made one clear decision for myself or shared honestly with one other person or owned one feeling or behavior instead of blaming. Each small practical step helped me experience the truth that God was with me and in me and would provide all I needed if I turned to him.

The practical questions wives have as they begin to deal with the news of sexual infidelity tend to fall into three broad categories:

> *Questions about your spouse.* These questions involve coming to terms with what a straying spouse has actually done and how best to respond to that reality.

> *Questions about your children.* These questions concern how children are affected by the betrayal, if the couple has children.
>
> *Questions about yourself.* These questions relate to the strong and sometimes overwhelming personal emotions that surface in the aftermath of betrayal.

The rest of this chapter will explore these issues one at a time. If a particular question doesn't concern or apply to you, skip it and go on to the ones that do.

Questions about Your Spouse

New information about a spouse's betrayal is always shocking. You may feel inundated with questions about his problems and your reality. Let's look at some of the most common questions.

Does My Husband Have a Sexual Addiction?

One of the first questions most wives face is in regard to what exactly they are dealing with in terms of their husband's betrayal. In some cases, a husband has committed a single act of sexual sin. In other cases, his behaviors may be indicative of a sexual addiction. The difference is that isolated incidents of sexual sin can be stopped fairly easily if there is intent to stop. Addiction, however, entails qualities of progression, tolerance, and an inability to stop despite a desire to do so. Addictive behavior indicates a need to "medicate" painful feelings.

As with alcohol or drug addiction, sexual addiction starts slowly and builds—either by adding new behaviors or by increasing the involvement with a particular behavior. If masturbation was discovered at an early age, it may have been used once or twice a month. Progression, then, would mean that over time, masturbation might increase to once a week and then once a day. Some sex addicts masturbate multiple times a day, even to the point of inflicting physical harm on themselves.

In addition, since active addiction leads to tolerance, more of the actual behavior is going to be needed to create the same "high" over time. We know this to be true with alcohol—where several drinks may have easily created a high when drinking first began, much more alcohol is needed to create that same feeling after months or years of chronic drinking. In much the same way, sexual thoughts and rituals create neurochemicals in the brain such as adrenalin, dopamine, and seratonin. All of these contribute to the high that sex addicts experience and then chase. The neurochemistry of the brain adjusts to the increased levels of neurochemicals over time, and more and more sexual thought and behavior are needed to create the same euphoric feeling.

Many sexual behaviors carry risky consequences. Despite the possibility of losing jobs, losing money, losing marriages, sex addicts continue to act out sexually. Many wives will say to me, "I don't know how he could be so crazy as to watch pornography while sitting at his desk at work. Anyone could walk in on him!" Or, "Didn't he think I would smell perfume on his clothes when he has been with her again and again?" Or, "I don't know how he could think I wouldn't see the credit card bill sooner or later—he has been charging all kinds of stuff that I would question." The behavior doesn't make sense—and that describes what the first step in the 12-step program calls "unmanageability": we keep doing something despite the negative consequences that could and do occur.

If you find out information about an affair, pornography use, or some other sexual acting out, your husband might quickly decide to stop what he was doing, ask for forgiveness, and agree never to do it again. If he is struggling with an addiction, however, his attempts to stop won't work. Mark attempted to get help in the first few years of our marriage by confessing involvement with another woman to his supervising therapist. He was told, "All men struggle this way. Don't mention anything about your behavior to Deb—it will just hurt her. And don't ever do it again." Mark took the therapist's advice to keep his behavior a secret, with all good intentions to be a faithful husband. But the behavior continued—and worsened—until years later he was confronted with disaster. Good men fall and don't stop, not because they don't want to and not always because they haven't tried. An addiction is about losing the power to stop despite all efforts to do so.

Mary told me her husband had had an affair during their first year of marriage. Although she was brokenhearted, they agreed to go to counseling to get help. She said their relationship improved after counseling, and she assumed the problem was resolved. Eight years later she found him in another affair, and he confessed to having used pornography their entire married life as well as having been involved with several other women. What appeared to have been a onetime fling was actually a full-blown addiction.

Joann's husband had been experimenting with pornography for years. She finally said she was fed up with it and told him she thought he had a sexual addiction. He denied it was a problem—he was just a typical man—and brought in a garbage bag to gather up all of the magazines, videos, and sex toys he had accumulated. He told her, "I'll show you I don't need this stuff. I'm throwing everything out." After several months, she found him surfing the Internet for pornography and also found phone bills with phone sex charges. Obviously, he couldn't stop his behavior.

Sexual addiction is also a means of coping with painful feelings. In chapter 3 we will take a closer look at coping mechanisms and the kinds of feelings that might be "medicated" with sexual sin.

Should I Leave or Stay?

Many women ask me if they should leave or ask their husband to leave after learning of his betrayal. Some believe he needs this kind of punishment to reinforce the fact that he has done a horrible thing. Others are simply so mad they can't stand the thought of sharing the same space with him, at least for a while.

Making a decision to leave because you need time to think things over or asking him to leave because you need space to sort through your pain is an example of acting out of your feelings and needs, not out of revenge. By the way, I am not a huge advocate for separation, especially when children are involved. If it is possible for both of you to take sexual betrayal seriously, it is not absolutely necessary to separate to work through your issues.

While there may be circumstances in which separation is necessary for a time, separation is not necessary to make progress in healing from betrayal. Some relationships are very toxic; in other words, verbal or physical battling occurs and thus safety is a concern. The only way to stabilize the environment is to create space between the two people. Even if space is needed, you can create that space with an "in-house" separation. You can choose to live in separate bedrooms for a while, live on separate floors if that is possible, decide to exclude certain topics of conversation without help from a trained third party, or decide not to socialize or take family trips together while you seek to heal. Couples can get very creative about honoring separate space for the purpose of individual reflection and growth. I've seen such separation provide enough salve to allow deep wounds to begin to heal.

Janet and Jeffrey have agreed on an in-house separation because they were reacting to each other in such a toxic way that they couldn't have a conversation about anything. Everything led to an argument. Resentments were building. Sex didn't feel safe for Janet, and in fact at times she was concerned for her physical safety because Jeffrey's anger was escalating. After they had undergone a month of in-house separation, Mark and I met with them. They both were decidedly more serene. While they hadn't been talking much during those weeks, staying focused on living in their own space had decreased their expectations of each other. When they weren't putting as much energy into getting each other to meet expectations, they became more aware of their own feelings and needs and sought to take care of those. After that month, they were beginning to be ready to have more conversation and interaction with each other. The separation had proven to be helpful in giving them space to detoxify from the relationship for a time.

Of course, the more dramatic form of separation is an out-of-house separation. It is more expensive, it can be more difficult on families with children, and it can distance you enough that being alone begins to feel much too comfortable. But if you really use the time away for the purpose of individual growth, reflection, and prayer, it can be a powerful tool for recovery. I have seen couples separate for several months and, while doing so, seek safe community for themselves, take time for meaningful reading and Bible study, and engage in individual therapy to examine their lives. The goal is to rest, restore, and prepare for return to the relationship. This kind of intentional time away can be very healing.

If there is enough support to navigate difficult conversations, it is often best for a couple to live together. Only by facing the ways you trigger and interact with each other can you practice making changes. If you live apart, it can become easy to conclude that life is much better without your partner, and you might convince yourself that the real problem is that you married the wrong person. However, character develops and intimacy grows as you face your triggers and work out new patterns of relating. You need a partner to do that! And by the way, the ways you cope and communicate will not change just because you change partners. As one renowned stress-reduction expert puts it, "When it comes right down to it, wherever you go, there you are."[1] Make a decision on living arrangements that will give you a chance to examine your life—not just run away from yourself and the person who has wounded you.

Consequences—Should I Create Them?

I recently talked with a woman who found her husband in bed with a colleague from work. After questioning him, she found out it wasn't the first time. Add to that her knowledge of his lifelong pornography use, and she was convinced that he had a serious problem. She told me about what he was doing and wasn't doing. She felt he was committed only marginally to recovery and wanted to know if that was normal. She expressed no emotions as she talked. She even mentioned that when she found her husband naked with the other woman, she calmly sat at the end of the bed and just talked to him about it. She didn't get angry, she said, and she didn't demand anything. She just asked some questions. She was frustrated when the next day he went back to work with the same employee sharing his office, but she accepted his explanation that he didn't want to arouse suspicion by firing the woman. "I can't believe it!" she told me. "He didn't even have any consequences after sleeping with another woman!" Unfortunately, he didn't even experience the natural consequence of seeing the sadness or anger of his own wife.

Consequences can impact our reactions and choices. It isn't unusual for a man to be complacent about his need to get help or make changes in his life if consequences have been minimal. If he hasn't lost his job, lost a lot of money, lost his family, or been arrested or publicly humiliated about embarrassing behaviors, he may not feel enough pain to seek change. Pain is what drives most of us to get help. Fear of consequences also leads us to want to change.

When Mark was fired and then publicly humiliated by front-page articles about his behavior, he and I both were in a lot of pain. At the time, I hated every minute of it. It seemed about as bad as it could get. Yet today I can see the blessing in that total crash-and-burn experience. His commitment to recovery was 100 percent. The diagnosis of sexual addiction seemed like a terminal disease. He was going to war with this illness. And in much the same way, I had my own battle to wage.

Those who have few consequences will be reluctant to commit to everything that true recovery and redemption will entail. "I promise I'll never do it again!" you might hear. "I realize I made a mistake, and I promise to change. I just don't want anyone to think I have a problem, that I'm not normal. I don't want my career to be in jeopardy." And so the talking goes. Until a decision has been made to get out of isolation and accept personal brokenness, there will be no permanent change. Many wives I've talked with tell me they knew about prior sexual sin and believed their husband was going to stop. Thus, they did nothing more, and he did nothing more. And months or years later, the behaviors returned or worsened.

As a wife who has been betrayed, you create the most natural consequence out of your feelings and needs. Problems will arise if you're not in tune with your own feelings. In my case, although the pain of my circumstances led me to tears and anger, I was also capable of cutting myself off from my emotions at times. I can't tell you how many wives I've talked with who barely showed emotion when recounting their stories. The most honest consequence our spouse can experience from us is an accurate expression of how we feel. Many women will rage or blame or throw out threats. Others will show up with overflowing compassion and patience. But somewhere under both of those responses is a lot of sadness and grief. Those are emotions that your husband can take in. Those remind him of the precious heart he has harmed.

Joanna was livid that her husband had purchased pornographic videos to watch while she was out of town visiting family. Since she was the sole income provider for the family, she responded by denying him access to any of "their" money, and she also determined how much cash he would have each week. This punishment only fueled his anger and his blaming of her controlling nature. It didn't serve Joanna well either: the consequence didn't change her husband's behaviors.

Antoinette's spouse struggled to stop looking at pornography. He was making better decisions, but he hadn't completely stopped his hurtful behaviors. Antoinette was an understanding wife. She was reasonable and patient and always tried to see the positive aspects of his efforts. She rarely cried or got angry—she worked very hard to be a gracious Christian woman. But after her husband acted on and then tried to cover up his behaviors several more times after his initial disclosure, her sadness and hopelessness overcame her. She couldn't go on with life like that anymore. Even if she had wanted to fake it and look okay to the outside world, she couldn't do it. Her authentic lifelessness and despair were excruciating for her husband to see. The consequence of possibly losing his wife and family led him to an important decision—he would get professional treatment and embrace recovery at the deepest level.

Some women will want to create consequences for their husband simply because he has done a bad thing and they believe he needs to be punished or he will do it again. But choosing punishing behaviors just for the sake of reprimanding your husband never works. Check your motivation: if you are sharing your feelings and making decisions to take care of yourself, you are being authentic. Consequences born of authenticity are the ones most likely to have an impact.

How Can I Make Sure He Deals with His Problem?

Mark's consequences were so devastating that he was prepared to get help. He readily allowed other men to help him. As I look back today, I see that his willingness to get help was a real gift to me. Unfortunately, not every woman has this experience. While you may have caught your husband with pornography or in an affair or he may have been found out by someone else, he still might not accept the need to get help.

After you have been hurt by his betrayal, you may start demanding that he see this therapist or go to that meeting, and if he's going once a week, you'd like him to go twice or three times. Out of your pain and anxiety to get back to some sort of normalcy in your life, you of course want to get everything moving more quickly than it is. Believe me, this sense of urgency is common and understandable.

Such urgency, however, creates a danger similar to driving on the highway with someone tailgating you. Surely you've experienced that annoying, demanding situation. I don't know about you, but when that happens to me, I want to do one of three things: step on the pedal and tear away, slow down and make my tailgater suffer longer, or slam on my brakes and make him pay. None of my responses gives my tailgater what he wants.

Consider whether your sadness or anger is turning you into a tailgater. Are you riding on your husband so much that he can't own his decisions about how he will get help? If he makes decisions simply to appease you, those decisions will only create frustration and anger directed toward you—not honest, useful reflection about himself and what he has done. The focus gets stuck on the wrong person and can actually delay the process of healing.

I can sense your anxiety growing. If you can't bump him along, then what can you do? You don't have to sit back and do nothing. That's our black-and-white thinking: either I'm all over him, controlling his every move, or I don't say anything! There are alternatives. You can learn to state your feelings: "I'm really hurt and angry about what you've done." And you can ask for what you need: "I need for us to find help to work through this. Are you willing?" And you can have consequences: "I don't know what I will need to do if there is no action, but I know I can't live with this pain. I'm sure I will be led to the next step, though."

If I Don't Control Him, Won't He Just Do This Again?

One concern that many women face is how much control to exert over a spouse who has admitted to inappropriate sexual behavior. There are many ways we wives seek to keep tabs on our wandering husbands: checking his phone bills, searching for the computer sites he has visited, driving to his workplace to make sure he is there, removing cable stations with promiscuous content, taking all of the computers out of the house, traveling with him on all of his business trips, not letting him go to the store alone, insisting that he "report in" every time he returns home regarding whether he has done anything "bad" today, and watching his eyes to see whether they are gazing inappropriately at other women. As one woman said to me, "I need to keep him on a tight leash!"

If you find yourself wielding some of these controlling behaviors, I want to encourage you to let go of your husband's recovery process. If you will not or cannot give up your role of Director of Husband Security, he will continue to find ways to sneak around your devices. Worst of all, you will look, feel, and sound like his mother, not his wife. You don't want to be in that role, because it will neither stop his behaviors nor help you build true intimacy with your husband.

Occasionally I've seen men attempt to keep their wives in the role of their mother. A frustrated woman in my group reported that her husband willingly confesses to her after everything he does. He looks and feels repentant and free after telling her, just as a little boy might feel after being honest with his mom. But Carol feels furious and justified in creating consequences for him so that he'll learn that his behavior is unacceptable. He, in turn, becomes angry that she wants to punish him. This pattern repeats itself several times every week.

Because this system wasn't working to stop his acting out or to create closeness for them, I suggested to Carol that she disengage herself from this dynamic and from her role as her husband's mother. I asked her to have him confess his sexual sin to the men in his support group. They would help hold him accountable for what he was doing. The women in Carol's group would help her deal with the anger or anxiety that arose for her.

Accountability is a practical way to sort out who oversees behaviors. Safe men in Mark's groups were there to remind him, encourage him, and/or confront him about the changes he wanted to make in his life. His first goal was to be sexually pure. Likewise, I had women helping me be accountable for my actions, words, and choices. When both you and your husband are in so much pain, you can't expect him to have objective, noncharged reactions to the things you say and do. If no one else is helping each of you make changes, you become that judgmental, critical voice inside your husband's head—the controller. He gets stuck in the role of child, feeling as if a parent is ruling his life. Neither of you can find intimate connection in this place. Thinking you can oversee your husband's behaviors by yourself is the greatest mistake you can make. The second biggest mistake is thinking you can single-handedly oversee your own changes. You need other safe women in your life to help you make changes, and your husband needs other safe men.

There is another important reason to give up control of your husband's behaviors. When other men step in to be accountability partners for your husband, he is empowered to own his journey of growth and purity. If you must control, manipulate, create fear, or withhold love to get perfect behavior from your husband, then what you do receive from him won't be authentic. Only when he *chooses* to love and honor you will you be able to receive what he gives as genuine love and nurture.

What Are Some Bottom Lines?

Bottom lines are behaviors that become deal breakers in your relationship. They are behaviors that you can no longer live with or tolerate in your marriage. They don't always have to be sexual in nature. Many wives I talk with are actually far more hurt by the lies and deception than they are by the infidelity.

Tracy's husband had an affair and refused to see a therapist with her. He wanted to convince her that it was over and he would never do it again. Her bottom line was that he get professional help to understand what drove him to an affair. CeeCee's bottom line was that her husband disclose all of his acting-out behaviors to her. She felt confused and distraught because the whole truth hadn't been revealed. She needed complete honesty to sort out the reality of her life. Hillary could no longer tolerate her husband's leaving for hours or even days without telling her where he was going. Cheryl's bottom line was that she wouldn't stay with her husband if he had another affair.

When you decide to establish a bottom line for your husband, you need to be willing to follow through. You need to know what it is you are going to do. Many times, I hear open-ended bottom lines: "I won't put up with you watching pornography anymore." "I can't stand your lying to me ever again." "I won't live with you hawking other women." But no consequence accompanies these pronouncements. It reminds me of my attempts to be tough as a parent. I could easily talk about what I did or didn't want one of the kids to do, but following through with a consequence was the hard part. They tested my bottom lines, and naturally so. It was a challenge to me to get clearer about what I needed and what I would do if my bottom lines weren't respected.

Do you sometimes feel your husband is testing your bottom line? You need to be clear about the consequence, and you need to be prepared to follow through. That's where many of us get hooked in some way. You might notice a pattern for yourself: "I've always had a hard time following through." "I'm not good at conflict." "I don't like to see people in pain."

Many times Brandy watched her husband leave the house after an argument, returning many hours or even several days later. She pleaded with Luke that he not abandon her and their young son, but he chose to leave anyway. Finally she demanded that if he left again, they were "done"—that was her bottom line.

Brandy was so afraid that she would become a single mom that she continued to welcome Luke back home despite her bottom line. This scenario had repeated itself so many times that her bottom line became worthless. Luke knew that there was not going to be any follow-through for the threats he heard.

If you want to establish a bottom line, you must be willing to do what you say you are going to do. For most of us, that is very hard to do.

You need to be aware that bottom lines can promote more lying. If your consequence is that you will leave or divorce, your husband might be so afraid of what will happen that he'll once again cover up, lie about, or deny his hurtful behaviors to prevent the outcome. And then the dynamic repeats itself in your relationship: you demand something; he becomes afraid and hides the truth; you become furious that he isn't being honest; he either gets angry or withdraws; and you feel hopeless that the situation will ever change.

There are alternatives to the black-and-white demands of bottom lines—the options are more "gray." You might say, "I'm not sure what I'll do when _____; I only know that I won't live with the pain it creates for me anymore." Gabrielle talked to Phillip about her concerns: "I have been very angry about the lies you have told me. If you lie again, I'll really need to take some time to decide what I'll do. It's very important to me that we can be truthful in our marriage." Unfortunately, Phillip did lie again a few months later, and Gabrielle was then faced with a decision. She decided she wasn't willing to keep working on the marriage unless he joined her in counseling to address the cause of his lying.

Trusting in yourself means that if and when your husband's destructive behaviors happen again, you will revisit your feelings and needs and consciously decide what your next step will be. Perhaps you will have more education about something by then, or more understanding about your own woundedness and triggers in a certain situation. Being more "gray" allows you to adjust to your journey as you continue to grow and do things differently.

What Boundaries Do I Need?

We all need boundaries in our lives. Boundaries help us determine who is responsible for what—not just material things, but feelings, thoughts, attitudes, behaviors, and choices.[2] Not only do boundaries help us allow good things to come in, but they also keep bad things out. Some of us have too many boundaries—or walls—that keep many good things out. The way I often keep very busy to soothe myself or keep from getting bored can wall off other people by sending the message that I'm unavailable. I can also choose to be passive or walk away, which is really to avoid having a boundary at all. The truth is, I may be afraid of conflict, so rather than create a safe boundary for myself, I abandon myself and do nothing.

One of my boundaries is refusing to sign any legal documents that I haven't read or don't understand. A new boundary is agreeing to accept work only if it allows me plenty of time with my family. You may have boundaries about physical safety: no one is allowed to touch you in inappropriate ways. Or you may have a fence that keeps out personal putdowns or swearing or yelling. In the same way that you create boundaries for your actions, your husband must set boundaries for his behaviors. You can't control them. You can be in charge only of the actions you will take when someone else's lack of boundaries causes you potential harm.

By now you can probably see the way that bottom lines and boundaries dovetail. You can't control the behaviors your husband engages in, but you can decide to do something different for yourself. Your feelings, thoughts, attitudes, behaviors, and choices are what you are responsible for. You can control only yourself, not anyone else. One of the first ways you can empower yourself with a new boundary is to acknowledge your feelings: "*I feel happy, sad, angry,*" and so on, rather than "*You make me* angry!" Owning your feelings means making "I" statements rather than "you" statements. Try it out—the change is such a simple one, but it creates a 180-degree shift in who is responsible.

Should I Protect Myself Financially?

Family money is often used to participate in phone sex, pay for cybersex, buy pornographic material, contract lap dances, massages, or prostitutes, or purchase gifts for affair partners. Sometimes thousands of dollars have been squandered away in these practices, all without your knowledge. If after your husband's disclosure you are not convinced his unhealthy behaviors have stopped and you believe the financial stability of your family is at risk, you may need to make decisions to protect yourself. Your debt incurred as a couple is debt that will be shared, even if your relationship doesn't last. You may need to seek legal advice to understand the consequences of out-of-control spending or a spouse who won't commit to getting help.

In general, you would be wise to take stock of what you know about money, how to manage it, where your money is, and what it is being used for. I know countless wives who delegate all monetary decisions to their husbands. They know very little, if anything at all, about their family's financial affairs. And then when crisis hits, they are helpless. If you are one of those women, it is *your* job to get involved. You need to know. Your signature is required for any number of financial transactions—taxes, loans, and credit card obligations, to name a few. If you are to make responsible decisions, you must be informed. A victim will relinquish her power to someone else and then be frustrated and angry that she has no choices. When it comes to family finances, you do have choices.

Questions about Your Children

Those of us with children have a powerful instinct to protect them from all harm. In light of sexual betrayal, we want to know how our children may be affected and what we should do.

What Do I Tell the Kids?

Although I had no idea of the "right" thing to say to the children, I knew they couldn't be oblivious to the pain I was in and the heaviness in our home. After Mark returned from treatment, we sat down with all of the kids and he told them in a general way that he had been sexually unfaithful to me. But before that disclosure, I wanted to acknowledge the pain in our home. I decided to tell them that Dad went away for a few weeks to get help. I told them he wasn't feeling good about himself and some things he had done and he needed help to sort out those issues. I also reminded them that we loved them and would always take care of them. At ages ten, six, and four, they were amazingly resilient and cooperative. Telling them that I was sad but was getting help was important to keep them from feeling as though they had to take care of me.

To this day, we have ongoing conversations about our story, encouraging any questions our children have. We are also honest about getting professional help and support them to do the same with their struggles.

Are My Children Safe?

The protection of our children is usually foremost in mothers' minds. While Mark's sexual behaviors included pornography and other women, they never extended to a connection with children. As I sorted out all of the new information after his disclosure, however, I needed to ask very directly if he had ever been inappropriate with our kids or others. I simply didn't know what was possible with the double life he had lived. I nervously awaited his reply, not sure what I would do if he said yes. Fortunately, he assured me that his sexual sin involved only adults. I suppose I could have doubted those words, because after all, he had been lying to me for years! But after witnessing the total brokenness of his character, I was quickly learning to trust my intuition and his heart. Otherwise, I definitely would have been more reluctant to trust any information he offered.

If you know for a fact that your husband has touched, penetrated, or inappropriately connected in some way with your children or any children, you should ask him to move out of your home immediately. You will need to speak with your pastor or therapist regarding how to report your husband's behavior to the appropriate local authorities. The law in all states requires that inappropriate sexual contact with children must be reported.

Many women who are in relationships with sex addicts have experienced sexual abuse themselves. If you are one of those, you will certainly be more sensitive to the possibilities of abuse in your home. Recently I received an email from a wife struggling with her "irrational fears," as she called them. Even though her husband has only looked at pornography, she wonders if his behaviors could progress to involve hurting children. She is aware that her own sexual abuse may be tainting her perception of reality. If you worry as this wife does, you can take time to explore with a therapist whether your anxieties are coming from your own life experiences. You may also ask your husband to get professional testing to see if he is telling the truth or has any propensity to act out with children.

The number of sex addicts who abuse children is extremely small. Ultimately, however, you may not feel completely safe until you ask your husband to get assessed for any predisposition or vulnerability he might have to the abuse of children. Many psychologists are trained to do these evaluations, generally referred to as psychosexual screening. Such testing can be presented to your husband as a helpful and positive boundary. You might say, "I want to trust you, and I want our family to be whole and to feel safe. It would be very helpful to me if you would get tested. I want us to be the best parents we can be. I need you to do this."

Questions about Yourself

Sexual betrayal feels like a personal attack—it is a wound that pierces the soul. Many questions arise concerning how to react and what decisions to make when personal emotions are confusing and overwhelming.

Should I Be Sexual with My Spouse?

The decision of whether to be sexual with your husband after the disclosure of infidelity is an important one. When Mark was in treatment, the therapists contracted with all patients to be abstinent for ninety days. Abstinence meant that you were not to be sexual with yourself or others (including your spouse). Being sexual referred to having an orgasm, not necessarily to hugging, kissing, or other physical expressions. When I arrived for Family Week, I was actually double-minded that this "assignment" was established. Although I was hurt and disgusted that Mark had been with other women, I also needed reassurance that he was attracted to me and still chose me. On the other hand, his constant pressure to be sexual was paralyzing for me at times, and I was relieved to know I would have a break from the pressure. My mixed feelings continued!

This decision is one that you may have to confront immediately after the disclosure. Will you agree to sexual contact with your husband just to keep the peace? Some wives are afraid to say no, even after their husbands have been unfaithful, because they are afraid of his anger when he is turned down. Other wives make a decision to be available whenever they are asked because they feel it is their Christian duty to do so. Still others may submit because it is at least *some* way of feeling connection with their husband. None of these reasons is healthy, and none will serve you in finding healing from sexual betrayal. None of them will give you authentic intimacy in your relationship. None will prevent your husband from acting out again. Changing the sexual pattern in your relationship will create a reaction—usually a negative one. The vision for healthy sexuality is that your yesses will truly mean yes and your noes will mean no, so that the love you share when you say yes is congruent with your heart. Any couple seeking to experience real intimacy must allow each other the freedom to say no and the assurance that they won't be punished when they do.

If your husband has come home to you asking to be sexual after unprotected sex with others, he has literally taken your life into his hands. Sexually transmitted diseases are rampant. If you want to know that you are free of disease, you will need to get tested by medical professionals. You must require your husband to do the same. If he doesn't consent to that precaution, you will need to make a decision for yourself about being sexual with him. It is your body, and you are responsible for it.

How Quickly Should I Forgive Him?

Another practical question that many wives face is how quickly to forgive their husband for his behavior. Although I'll talk about forgiveness in detail in a later chapter, I want to take a moment to caution you against rushed forgiveness. Many devout Christian women will want to forgive quickly because they feel God has directed them to do so. And I believe some women hurriedly offer forgiving statements because they long to get back to "normal" or put painful experiences behind them. Forgiving can feel like forgetting or denying in this rushed state, and I've never seen it work to heal the pain of betrayal in the long term.

I've also seen husbands caught in sexual sin demand that their wives forgive them, blaming them for not honoring Christian teaching when they don't. When husbands demand forgiveness in this way, they also seem to want their wives to let go of any feelings they may have. If she is still sad or angry or confused, he gets impatient or distant. "I thought you forgave me," he might say. Pain doesn't go away with these quick attempts to forgive. Pain stored in your heart and body will only surface in time to damage any temporary serenity you might have achieved.

Forgiveness is a process, not a onetime event. Just deciding to stay and grapple with the painful reality of betrayal is a part of forgiveness. It is the first step of a complex process, which we'll look at in depth in chapter 8.

In Whom Should I Confide?

Telling your story will inevitably create anxiety, for knowing who to tell and what to tell them is very difficult. Except for notifying my best friend and my parents, I initially kept Mark's double life a secret. Oh, I almost forgot—the whole city knew because of the newspaper articles! In reality, though, the complete truth about Mark's story was not revealed publicly. I did have a choice to share with others, but frankly, I wasn't very motivated in the beginning to tell anyone. I felt a great deal of shame about the nature of sexual sin. I felt no one would accept Mark or me if I talked. Fortunately, I was able to attend Family Week and then my therapy group, where I could begin sharing. If I hadn't had those outlets, I'm sure my obsessive thoughts and hopelessness would have grown to unmanageable proportions.

Who are you talking to? Is there anyone who can know the entire nature of your story? I'll often hear a woman say her husband has refused to let her tell anyone about his sin. He would be too embarrassed. He wouldn't want anyone to talk about him. His career might be jeopardized if the wrong person heard. I advocate that a betrayed woman needs to have someplace to go and talk. If you are in this situation, I ask you to think about some safe women who would be trustworthy and able to keep a confidence. Determine your motivation for sharing with each of these women. If you can honestly say that it isn't for revenge, that it isn't to take sides against your husband, and that you desire to grow your relationship with this woman, then she is probably a safe person with whom to share. Other characteristics of a safe woman include the following: she is a good listener and doesn't try to fix your situation; she doesn't judge your decisions; she is vulnerable about adversity in her own life; she affirms your efforts; she respects your desire not to share at times and doesn't pressure you; and she doesn't use your confidences to feel prideful in her relationship with you. Do you have safe women like this in your life? You can't sit in isolation and expect yourself to be sane. Eventually you will drop into sadness, depression, and possibly despair. Your body will take on the feelings that you are not able to process and cope by shutting down in some way.

What Is My Body Saying to Me?

Our bodies carry much of what is going on in our lives. I woke up one Saturday morning as Mark was packing to leave town for a conference. It was exactly one month before the living room disclosure session. I had no idea of the double life that was to be revealed, yet I do believe that in some way, my body knew something about what was coming. While making the bed that Saturday morning, the right side of my body went completely numb — it was paralyzed. It didn't have that tingly feeling you sometimes get from sitting on your leg too long; my arm hung loosely at my side, and I collapsed as I tried to walk on my leg. I tried to call out to Mark, but my tongue wasn't functioning either, and only garbled noises croaked out of my mouth. He must have heard something, because in a moment he rushed into the room to find me sitting on the side of the bed with panic in my eyes.

The transient ischemic attack (TIA) was a short-lived stroke of sorts, and in ten minutes or so it began to clear its way out of my system. While my fine motor actions weren't perfected for several hours, I was relieved that other feelings were returning. I was directed to go straight to the hospital, where for three days I was subjected to numerous brain and heart tests. I heard shouts of "STAT" often, which I now know meant I was in a health crisis. The doctors found nothing except possibly a faint mitrovalve prolapse. To this day I've never experienced that combination of symptoms again.

I was only thirty-seven years old and in the best physical shape I had ever been in. I asked what could have caused this TIA — was it stress or some psychological problem? The doctors simply had no answers. I learned more about the distress of holding feelings in and the way that repressed emotions can manifest themselves in physical symptoms. I asked my friend and ER physician if he thought it was possible to have this kind of attack from suppressed feelings. He agreed that it was very possible. He and his colleagues had actually done research on codependency and its manifestation in physical ailments, and he shared their findings with me.

I knew in that moment that my body had been aware of what my intellect hadn't even known yet. In my place of isolation, my body was screaming out to me in pain. A part of me knew something was wrong, but I chose not to acknowledge it. I did what was familiar to me — I withdrew. Even today, when I withhold pressing feelings and don't find a way to talk about them, the same arm that was paralyzed will begin to quiver. It is my stark reminder not to ignore the need to speak up.

Is your body talking to you in some way? Is there something you need to stop ignoring or minimizing or justifying? Do you need to explore your physical aches and pains?

Do I Have to Make a Commitment?

"I'm so confused," you might be saying, "that I don't know what I want. Sometimes I feel like I just can't do this, and other times I know I love him so much that I do want to work it out." If you feel as though you're on a roller coaster, you share the same feelings of every wife I've met. In the first days, weeks, and months after the disclosure of betrayal, you've probably had conflicted feelings about what you will do. One concern I have for wives is that they not make a major decision to leave their husband when they are in the middle of chaos and deep emotional pain. It is such an easy time to leave; after all, none of us likes to be in pain.

I want to encourage you to wait awhile before making a choice whether to end your relationship. Rarely are good decisions made in the midst of emotional crisis. If you take the time to get support and to examine what is going on in your life, you'll be more likely to make a decision you won't regret later. Can you decide that for a specific period of time you won't leave your marriage? That time frame may be only a month, or it may be six months or a year. It doesn't mean a lifetime! But it does mean you will honor your commitment — no threats to leave; no surprise divorce papers. It can be a difficult request if you feel this is the one way you gain power or seek to be heard. In my case, I used a subtle form of "leaving" by too often saying, "I don't know if I can stand this anymore." Although I never intended it to mean divorce, Mark heard it that way. Our conversations always came to an abrupt halt. Only when I agreed to stop making that statement did Mark begin to feel freer to talk about his real feelings.

At the end of your commitment, you can agree to revisit the decision to leave or divorce. In the meantime, it gives both you and your husband the freedom to be totally honest, knowing neither of you will be abandoned. The freedom to be honest won't exist if you don't feel safe; and if you're worried about someone leaving, you won't feel safe.

Baby Steps

When you are faced with the tragic news of infidelity in your marriage, you can feel so shocked and overwhelmed that you don't know what to do next. Most of us don't even know how to get through the next hour or day, let alone think about the months ahead. Thinking about and acting on practical things can be a helpful way to get started, a way of empowering yourself when you feel as though you have had every ounce of life kicked out of you. When you make one clear decision for yourself or share one honest feeling with a trustworthy person, life can start to flow back in. I encourage you to think small—just one step at a time, one day at a time. What is your most pressing need today? Believe that God is reaching for your hand right now to lead you to the next baby step.

Thinking It Over

1. Do you ever try to do detective work in your husband's life? If so, why do you find it difficult to stop looking for evidence of betrayal?

2. How do you allow others to hurt you? In what ways can you create safety (boundaries) for yourself?

3. Are you aware of walls you create to shut other people out of your life—walls such as raging, withdrawing, being a martyr, or not speaking up?

4. If you are experiencing physical pain or discomfort, what might your body be trying to tell you? Is it holding on to certain feelings, such as fear, anger, anxiety, or sadness?

5. What baby steps can you take to begin your journey of healing?

1. YES. ITs hard to stop because have this need to know. I need to see what he sees, what he writes, who he calls/texts. I don't want another surprise and have a need to be prepared for a potential next time. I want to create a wall to keep him out of my heart at times.

2. → others hurt me when I choose to let them in my heart and I don't create boundaries. I'm unsure how to create those safe places for myself.

3. I am aware that I want to withdraw from situations and just be in my head... which is too dangerous.

4. My hands are falling asleep now, but I was having nightmares about Chris' infidelity.

5. My baby steps include being w/ God more

CHAPTER 2

Why Should I Get Help When It's His Problem?

Accepting the Support You Deserve

Accept the gift you have given to so many. Let people love you back.

Jeanette Osias

In you, LORD, I have taken refuge; . . . Turn your ear to me, come quickly to my rescue; be my rock of refuge, a strong fortress to save me.

Psalm 31:1–2

When Mark left the sexual addiction treatment center, his case manager, Jeff, arranged for his "after care": the ongoing counseling that he would receive in our local area after treatment. Oddly enough, Jeff had an after-care plan for me, too. I was wondering if he misunderstood the basic issue here: *Mark was the one with the problem, not me!* Mark was the one who had broken our wedding vows and who had committed sexual sin; I was the one who was faithful, responsible, truthful, and righteous in all I did. Why in the world would I need to go to therapy?

My designated evening for women's group was Tuesday, and I agreed to go if it would help Mark heal. I didn't want to look defiant or angry. I didn't like the "codependent" labels the treatment center people were trying to give me, so I wanted to look cooperative and independent, making the decision to go because I thought it was a good idea. When I arrived for my group, it was probably for all the wrong reasons. Nevertheless, Maureen, my therapist, was gracious in welcoming me to the group and invited me to share my story with the other women. Despite the fact that my world had crashed just four weeks earlier and I was overwhelmed with anger, sadness, and uncertainty, I summarized my situation without one tear or emotional glitch. It felt like a victory. I had gotten through my introduction without falling apart. Maybe I wasn't such a mess after all! Maureen didn't comment on my emotional state one way or the other; she just welcomed me to the safe community of women and began encouraging me to experience my feelings—all of them.

I learned that participating in a healthy community of women is more than just being together and talking or doing something with women. It is a safe place where you can feel free to share all of your fears, frustrations, and behaviors. It is a place where you can open your heart, admit your inadequacies, own your mistakes, share your anger and grief, or just vent. You can be you, with all of your flaws, and still be accepted and encouraged and loved. In return, safe women will also share their stories, be vulnerable, and not try to fix you. They will listen to you, comfort you, and encourage you. That is safe community. It doesn't happen very often. Most people have no experience being in safe community. We more often manicure our appearance, adjust our attitude, and put on a smile so the world thinks we're fine, when on the inside we're falling apart.

After that first night of group, I knew I had found a "home"—a place where safe women and a very gifted therapist began leading me through my pain and hearing me like I had never been heard before. The experience was freeing. The authenticity modeled to me was contagious. For the first time in my life, my insides matched my outsides. What I said and how I looked reflected what I was feeling. When I was sad, I learned to allow myself to *be* with that feeling. I looked sad, and often I cried. When I was angry or frustrated or anxious, I learned how to talk about those feelings instead of hiding them away or busying myself with something else to do. Being congruent took a lot of practice, and my new safe community became my practice arena. I quickly claimed this place as mine—for me—for my healing and growth, no matter what happened to Mark or to our relationship.

Resistance to Getting Help

When life crashes after betrayal, the shock of it all can leave women paralyzed. It can also leave them angry, devastated, confused, ashamed, and resistant to outside support. See if you relate to any of the reasons the following women had for "keeping the family secret," distancing themselves from their pain, or taking a passive stance that kept them feeling stuck and isolated.

Jennie had no idea where to go for help. She didn't want to ask anyone because then she would have to admit that she had a serious problem. She felt stuck with the wreckage and shame of her life. She decided she would just have to figure out how to cope with her sorrow by herself.

Amiko was afraid to talk to anyone other than her family members. She had been taught all her life that she shouldn't air her dirty laundry outside her own family. The idea of talking to strangers about these sensitive issues was unthinkable.

Brenda's husband forbade her to tell anyone about what had happened. He was a prominent lawyer and couldn't risk anyone hearing about his behaviors. He claimed that it was his problem and it would embarrass him and possibly jeopardize his career if she shared his issues. She didn't like being told what she could or couldn't do, but she had to admit that she didn't want anything to happen to her husband's ability to provide for their family. She agreed to a conspiracy of silence.

Rosa's family didn't have a lot of money. Her husband was unemployed and she worked only part time. She said that since money was scarce, it was more important that her husband get help first. She would wait and see if things got better after that.

Gretchen had economic dilemmas, too, but they were entirely different from Rosa's. She and her husband were blessed with plenty of resources. However, she believed seeking out professional help when she hadn't tried long enough to solve her own problem would be a waste of money. Her husband had disclosed his infidelity just weeks earlier, and she convinced herself she must try harder to make things work before asking for support.

Cecilia had three children and worked two part-time jobs besides volunteering at church events. She couldn't imagine squeezing one more thing into her schedule. She decided that when the kids got older, she would have more time to devote to working out the problems between her and her husband. She was just too busy now to think about it.

Peg decided that it was her husband's problem, not hers, and she wouldn't waste her precious time complaining about her life to other women. She also wasn't willing to miss her golf outings with friends, book club evenings, and weekly Bible study to go to therapy sessions for "his" issue.

Caroline's husband was loved and admired by all of their friends. When he fell into sexual sin, they poured out sympathy on him and gave Caroline countless suggestions for how she could support him. She felt emotionally bypassed and even blamed for the whole mess. She couldn't identify her own needs, much less ask for them to be met. She felt like a victim, with no choices and nowhere to turn.

Robin thought that women who stayed with "these kinds of men" were just weak and dependent. She didn't want to be one of "those kinds of women," so she chose to pack up her hurt and confusion and leave her marriage without looking back.

Brianne was a pastor, a very public person in her community. She knew every therapist in her small town, and any support groups she might think about going to would likely be filled with people who knew her in her pastoral role. She felt there was no safe place where she could be anonymous and her issues would be kept confidential.

Resistance to the involvement of other people in the aftermath of sexual betrayal is common and understandable for any number of reasons, but remaining isolated with your pain and confusion is probably the worst thing you can do if you want to heal. When I came out from hiding and found other people who were willing to do the same, I began to heal. God uses other people to show us his grace, his comforting hand, his acceptance and love. Safe community becomes the place where we experience others with Jesus' skin on. It is the place where we learn to let go of controlling everything and expecting that we should be able to heal from all of our pain alone. It is the place where we can admit that we have problems and that having them is normal.

Initially I let the fact that I had been sexually betrayed make me feel abnormal and ashamed. But I didn't want to think of myself or my family as having "problems." "Normal people don't experience things like this," I would tell myself. But in his powerful book *Everybody's Normal Till You Get to Know Them*, John Ortberg examines some common misperceptions about "normal":

> We all want to look normal, to think of ourselves as normal, but the writers of Scripture insist that no one is "totally normal" — at least not as God defines normal. "All we like sheep have gone astray," they tell us. "All have sinned and fall short of the glory of God."[1]

He goes on to say:

> Have you ever noticed how many messed-up families there are in Genesis? Here is a quick summary: Cain is jealous of Abel and kills him. Lamech introduces polygamy to the world. Noah — the most righteous man of his generation — gets drunk and curses his own grandson. Lot, when his home is

surrounded by residents of Sodom who want to violate his visitors, offers instead that they can have sex with his daughters. Later on his daughters get him drunk and get impregnated by him—and Lot is the most righteous man in Sodom!... Abraham has sex with his wife's servant, then sends her and their son off to the wilderness at his wife's request. Jacob marries two wives and ends up with both of their maids as his concubines as well when they get into a fertility contest.... The writer of Scripture is trying to establish a deep theological truth: Everybody's weird.

Every one of us—all we like sheep—have habits we can't control, past deeds we can't undo, flaws we can't correct ... every one of us pretends to be healthier and kinder than we really are.... From the time of Adam in the Garden of Eden, sin and hiding have been as inevitable as death and taxes. Some people are pretty good at hiding. But the weirdness is still there. Get close enough to anyone, and you will see it. Everybody's normal till you get to know them.[2]

When you think about it, or have the opportunity to be a part of a group of people who are admitting to their "as is" tags, you see that everyone is struggling in some way. Only people who hide away a part of their lives can pretend to be normal.

Do you find yourself relating to any of the stories of the women described earlier in this section? They are all very strong, successful, and attractive women. If you met any one of them in your Bible study or in your neighborhood, you wouldn't consider them abnormal in any way. Just like you, however, they have parts of themselves that seem too scary to talk about, too unsafe to share with a world that often judges and rejects. Do you have a desire to be known and still be safe—to stop hiding from the authentic parts of you—problems and all? I pray you will find the courage to seek out the company of others who desire to tend to their hurt and confusion and struggles.

My closest friends used to be those I shared classes or activities with, other mothers whose children played with mine, or women I served with on church or school committees. While I thought I was close to them, I didn't begin to know what intimacy meant until I shared the pain and "weirdness" in my life with others doing the same. Doing so began a totally different experience of being connected to other women. Pain and honesty were the foundation of the development of authentic relationships.

I don't think I ever would have signed up for this journey of examining myself and growing more dependent on God if I hadn't been in enough pain. I liked controlling my life. I thought I was doing a fairly good job of being a woman, a wife, and a mother. I didn't see many problems with my character. I had no idea that God wanted more for me and that through the adversity of sexual sin he could take me on a trip of great discovery. The first step was deciding that I needed to participate in a process of uncovering my hurt and that I needed to trust the process — God's process for growing my character and healing my heart.

I hope I have convinced you that staying isolated or avoiding reality is not a solution to ridding yourself of the pain of betrayal. The feelings won't just go away over time. Not thinking about your husband's sinful decisions won't make them magically disappear. Quickly forgiving your husband and "moving on" will only bury your feelings of anger and sadness — only to have them seep out at unexpected times down the road. The better choice is to go to any lengths to get the support you deserve so you can heal and thrive, not just survive.

Three Components of Healing

The kind of help that will transform your pain has three critical components. To understand how essential each component is, imagine a three-legged stool. The stool represents your marriage, and each leg represents one vital component of the help you need to recover from sexual betrayal.

- 1. *My safe place.* The first leg is your safe place to share your feelings and work on your woundedness.

- 2. *His safe place.* The second leg is your husband's place to work on his consequences, trauma, feelings, and commitment to new behavior.

- 3. *Our safe place.* The third leg is a place where the two of you, as a couple, can talk about your ongoing issues, practice new ways of communicating, and share your insights about your own lives. It is also a place where you can hear each other's pain, grieve your losses, and create a new vision together.

All three legs are equally important. When one of the legs is missing, your stool does not stand. The stool represents a healthy marriage — a husband and wife emotionally and spiritually connected. Maintaining a strong and steady stool — a healthy relationship — requires making a commitment to all three essential components of healing.

While you can't control your husband's choices and whether or not he will seek help for himself, you can make a decision to get started yourself, even if you are the first to take the step. You don't need to wait for your husband. Your desire to grow through this pain doesn't require that he will as well. Your marriage may not be saved or become what you would like it to be if he chooses not to participate, but you can make choices that support your own growth.

I have seen women take first steps in many different ways. Sometimes a wife is fed up with sexual sin that will not stop and she simply is driven to do something; once she has made an appointment to get help, her husband then agrees to come along. Sometimes a woman comes alone for a long time, making many changes in her life; her husband may begin to believe that asking for help can make a difference, and he then engages in the process, too. Sometimes a woman begins a recovery process by herself and is never joined by her husband. Ideally, both decide to seek help together and trust that God will somehow use this adversity for growth in their marriage. In any situation, your first step to find healing will pay off—you will be a richer person for having taken time to examine yourself.

Doing something as unfamiliar as getting help for yourself can be very difficult. It can be even more difficult if you don't have a companion to join you. I want to assure you that any movement by either spouse has the potential to begin shifting the dynamics in your family system. Your family is like a mobile: if you tug on any part of the mobile, all of the other parts will move as well. If you are feeling stuck or paralyzed by sexual betrayal, your choice to get help can also begin the healing process for those around you.

Finding the Right Support

Emotional and spiritual support, wise counsel, and safe community can be found in a number of places. You may wish to go to your pastor first. He or she will often refer you to a professional counselor who can see you one-on-one. Counselors are educated in many ways. There is no specific degree that guarantees the best kind of help, and not all professionals know how to lead couples through the pain of sexual infidelity.

If you truly believe your marriage is worth fighting for, keep looking until you find help that works. Here are some questions you may want to ask anyone who may professionally help you (including your pastor):

- Have you worked with other couples dealing with sexual purity issues? Sexual addiction? If so, how many? Do you typically advise them to stay together?

- Do you recommend individual counseling as well as couples counseling?
- Are you familiar with any of these authors who write about sexual purity: Dr. Patrick Carnes, Dr. Mark Laaser, Dr. Dave Carder, Dr. Harry Schaumburg?
- Do you address family-of-origin issues?
- Do you endorse 12-step programs or support groups of any kind?

Mark and I have seen many people who have lost hope in their marriage because the "help" they received was ineffective. For example, Melissa visited a Christian counselor with her husband to discuss for the first time his involvement with pornography and prostitutes. After questioning them primarily about their sexual life, he turned to her and told her that she simply needed to be more sexual with her husband.

Nancy visited her pastor when her husband refused to get help. She was told that she must just have faith and pray more about their problem. If she had enough faith, God would change her husband.

When Kiesha and Damola went for their first counseling session, they were advised to start "dating" each other more often. The therapist's assessment was that they didn't get away from their children enough, and if they would simply concentrate on their relationship, they would feel connected again and Damola would no longer feel the need to break his marriage vows!

If you receive counsel or direction that doesn't feel helpful or right, trust your intuition and keep looking for the right fit. An effective therapist or support group will give you hope and practical tools for meaningful change and deep healing. I not only participated in a therapist-led group for eighteen months, but I also found safe community in 12-step groups. Both experiences were invaluable to my process of growth, and I can't recommend group support highly enough. Here are some of the kinds of groups you might find helpful.

Therapy group. A therapy group is a group led by a professional therapist. Its agenda may be one of "processing," meaning that the issues discussed are brought by the participants each week; or it may be more educational, involving lectures, book studies, or workbook lessons. Typically, the size of a therapist-led group is limited and a fee is charged that is sometimes reimbursed by insurance companies.

Church support group. A church support group is usually led by a lay leader, someone who has dealt with similar issues but is farther down the road to healing. These groups often use some kind of materials or workbooks to guide them through their meetings. Generally there is no fee or a nominal fee for participation, and often there is no limit to the number of group members.

Twelve-step group. A 12-step group helps participants look at their feelings and behaviors. They are also a source of rich community—people seeking to change and grow, all in the safety of anonymity. These groups are numerous and free. Following are some of the 12-step programs that might be helpful to you. (See the resources section at the end of this book for more information.)

- COSA (Codependents of Sex Addicts Anonymous)—for those whose lives have been affected by another person's compulsive sexual behavior.
- CODA (Codependents Anonymous)—for those who want to evaluate any patterns or characteristics of codependency in their relationships.
- Al-Anon—for those in relationship with an alcoholic. Although alcoholism may not be something you are experiencing in your family, this group can be very helpful in educating you about codependency issues in any relationship.
- OA (Overeaters Anonymous)—for those whose primary coping strategy is "medicating" with food. Many hurting spouses cope with their pain by overeating or by acting out

an eating disorder such as bulimia or anorexia nervosa. If you find that this is one way you have been managing your sadness, anger, and so on, OA may be a safe haven where you can find support and tools for healing.

Your own group. The idea of starting your own group might be a scary thought, but many women have found their most meaningful support by gathering with just one or two other women to work through a specific book or curriculum. I recommend the workbook *A L.I.F.E. Guide: Spouses Living in Freedom Everyday.*[3] You could also choose a book to read together. See the resources section at the end of this book. Ask your pastor or therapist if he or she knows someone else who is alone in the process of healing from sexual betrayal. Confidentially, he or she can connect people who are willing to work together. You can also attend 12-step meetings and listen for stories you identify with. You could then invite the women who share these stories to join a specific group for those who want to recover from betrayal.

Ask God to lead you to safe women who can be companions on your journey. I recently received an email from a woman I'd previously encouraged to find support. She writes, "I have learned so much about myself and why [sexual betrayal] has entered our lives. I have made some of the best friends I will ever have in my life. I now have others to encourage and to be encouraged by. I just wanted to thank you for encouraging me to begin my road to recovery."

Consider Yourself "In Training"

I love to play golf, and Tiger Woods is someone I admire and watch regularly. He has already won more major tournaments at his age than anyone in history. In an interview, he was asked the difference between being a very good player and being a great one. He responded, "Being able to repeat what you do." He was also asked why he changed his swing twice after all of his victories, to which he replied, "To get better. I'm building something here, and it takes time."

My own experience playing tennis has taught me some great lessons about what it means to build something worthwhile over time—to "train" for change and healing in myself and in my marriage. As part of my recovery process, I made a commitment to get back to a game I really loved but had never found time to play very much. I signed up for a few lessons and practices and then moved on to playing on a team with five other women. One week we practiced drills with our coach, and the next we played matches with other teams. After each match our coach critiqued our play. My coach was kind and encouraging, looking for those things I was improving while also noting strokes or strategies I needed to work on. I was actually a lot harder on myself than he was, disappointed that I could make shots in practice but then miss them in matches. I was really trying to be a good player. The truth was, I owned my own company and work was demanding, I had three children, and I was participating in recovery events. I could squeeze only so much time out of my schedule for this new venture.

My wise coach told me in those self-critical moments, "Debbie, you're a good player; you just need to hit thousands of balls until these strokes become so much a part of you that you don't even think about them anymore. It takes time and lots of training. You can't expect yourself to make great shots when you only have time to practice once a week."

Training versus Trying[4]

I knew that healing from the pain of sexual betrayal would require the same kind of practice and commitment required to improve my tennis game—it would require me to be in training. Just trying out a few therapy sessions or talking occasionally to a woman who understood me wasn't going to be enough.

We can deceive ourselves by telling ourselves we are doing more or trying harder than we actually are. We can be double-minded about our efforts—wanting very much to have the results of training, but not making the decisions to bring about those results. Old patterns are hard to change. The way we have communicated with our spouse, coped with our feelings, and managed to stay together amid secrets or signs of sexual impurity will be difficult to unbury and remodel. We are humans who seek familiarity. We do things the way we have seen them done. Just "trying" a few things to see if they "work" won't be enough. Often when life changes to feel "good enough," we stop seeking "greatness." We must commit to long-term training to develop new behaviors and healthier patterns of relating to others in order to transform our life.

I'm good at *trying* many things. The thrill of learning something new or growing in some way always motivates me to get started. But *training* is another thing. Training requires overcoming several obstacles. It takes time. It takes commitment and the reordering of priorities, because I can't be in training for too many things at once. It takes the understanding that training involves both highs and lows. It isn't always thrilling. In fact, training is just plain hard work. But the vision of what I ultimately desire is what keeps me going.

When taking first steps to find healing for myself, I needed to make a choice that I was going to be in *training*—not just halfhearted *trying*. I wanted change badly enough for *myself* that nothing was going to get in my way. I wasn't going to put in tremendous effort just because it might help Mark get better. I didn't know what the outcome of our marriage was going to be. I just knew from my initial participation in Family Week and then in my women's group that I had things to learn about myself. At age thirty-seven, I thought I had graduated from "How to Live Life." Now I could see that I was just poking around at what that meant. God probably likened me to a junior high student when it came to living an emotionally and spiritually healthy life. It was time for me to get into training.

Training Obstacles

One of the biggest obstacles I had to overcome when I began training for change was thinking I couldn't afford it. Since training doesn't usually provide instant evidence of progress, I could easily tell myself I was wasting my time and money. I like to see results—and the sooner the better. There's no denying that training comes at a cost. But here's another way to look at it: in more than twenty years of investing in my personal emotional health—being in training—I have spent less than many families would have spent on one or two elaborate family vacations. I would never exchange my long-term training experiences for those fleeting ones. And today, the return on my training investment is invaluable.

Recovery is an investment in your emotional health. It takes time, patience, and money. Are you willing to give those? Many women will excuse themselves from the opportunities to heal because they are too busy or too tired. If you were to be diagnosed with a chronic, debilitating disease, would you do what it takes to get well? Dealing with the pain of betrayal can eat away at your serenity and your character until you don't even recognize yourself. If you let it go untreated, it will begin to infect the whole of who you are. Can you afford to let that happen?

Training Partners

When people train *together*, they can be powerful allies for change. That's another reason committing to a safe community is so important to healing from sexual betrayal. The process of healing together builds trust—other people are there for you so you can share your feelings and be heard; they can support you through your decisions; they can practice with you new ways to relate to people; they can remind you of how many more "shots" you're making. Often our progress is noticed most by those watching us from the outside. When I'm in training, I often find it difficult to see the subtle changes that are occurring because I'm focused intently on the task at hand. So when someone validates my progress, I feel empowered.

If your husband decides to get help in the aftermath of his betrayal as well, the two of you can train together to transform your marriage. The choices you have been making as a couple have created many patterns in your relationship. What do you do when you are sad, angry, lonely, disappointed, or resentful? Do you figure out ways to exit the situation and be alone, or do you move in and attack the situation? How do you react when your husband is demanding, depressed, distant, or distracted by others (especially women)? How do you talk? Or do you remain silent? What do you need? Do you even know? How do you ask for your needs to be met? Or do you just assume he will read your mind?

Examining the way you interact in terms of your communication and behaviors will yield very helpful information. If both of you choose to explore these issues, you can begin to train for the vision of a newfound relationship. If your husband doesn't join you in this journey, you can train by yourself. Training and refining your character and behaviors will transform all of your relationships. You will have more authentic relationships with friends, children, colleagues, and God. If you move into a new love relationship, you won't bring the old destructive patterns that led to hiding, distancing, and despair. It is a win-win situation for you.

Training for Intimacy

During a group session, Kim related a painful story about her parents. Twenty years into their marriage, her father was sexually unfaithful to her mother. Kim said they went to counseling and that for a while things seemed to get better. Eventually, though, they divorced. She was very skeptical that the progress she and her husband, Tom, were making in the wake of his infidelity would last. She couldn't trust the shift that was happening in their closeness. When we talked about the similarities of her parents' situation, she began crying. She could see that their experience with "getting help" and then failing was all she knew. When I asked her specifically what she noticed about her parents' efforts to change, she said, "Well, actually, my dad [who had had the affair] worked very hard at going to counseling, asking forgiveness of my mom, repenting to church elders, and accepting their discipline and accountability. But now that I think about it, my mom wouldn't do anything. She refused to go get help for herself. And now she's remarried to a man fifteen years older than she is, and she's still a mess." Kim took a deep breath and sighed, taking in a new awareness: she was making a choice to deal with her husband's infidelity very differently. She had every reason to hope that she and Tom were in training for a long-lasting change in their patterns of relating that would unlock the door to the intimacy they both wanted.

After the disclosure of several affairs, Sun and her husband, Jung, worked hard in a recovery program for one year. Sun continued to go to her support group and work individually on her issues. Jung, however, fell away from his program when his job became more demanding. Eventually he fell into sin again and visited several prostitutes. When Sun found out, she knew that she wouldn't tolerate a husband who would not stay committed to her sexually. She filed for divorce. Her pain grew even greater with all of the changes in her life, but she leaned faithfully on her safe community and therapy. Sun was able to forgive Jung, and she continued to learn healthier communication skills. Today, she is a single mom, managing a new job and three young children. She has been able to create a home where her children are encouraged to love their dad and where there is cooperation in arranging shared parenting for them. Her home is not a place of bitterness. She is grateful for the tools she has gained that support emotional health in her life and the lives of her children.

Over 50 percent of marriages fail today. The statistic is no better for Christian couples. And for those leaving broken marriages
and attempting to find the "right" person without examining the
patterns of the broken relationship, the statistics climb even higher.
Most of us live with the illusion that if we choose the right partner,
we will be happy and content. If we're not, we often think we
just need to find someone else. The problem is that our patterns
of relating to others follow us no matter where we go, no matter
which partner we choose.

The best way I know to enrich my relationships is to know myself better and be well trained in the skills of emotional intimacy.
Intimacy is about connecting with someone emotionally and spiritually. It is not about merely sharing positive feelings or having
a great sexual connection. Intimacy means finding security in a
relationship that allows you to share all of your feelings, including
fear, anxiety, anger, disappointment, joy, hope, and so forth. In an
intimate and safe relationship, you trust that when you do share,
you will not be abandoned, criticized, or judged. That is a huge
vision for what a relationship can be—and such a relationship can
take a lifetime of training to develop.

Committing to a Redemptive Journey

The courageous steps of getting help, establishing safe community, and training for change are foundational for optimal spiritual
growth in the wake of sexual betrayal. You honor God and grow
spiritually every time you choose to grow through, rather than be
destroyed by, your pain.

The most important insight I had amid the crushing pain of
betrayal was that somewhere in that destruction of my life, there
was an opportunity to birth new character—to be more like Jesus.
When I committed to finding my way along that redemptive path
with a whole new kind of companionship—a community of safe
women and a husband willing to join me in the journey—I slowly

began to feel the changes within me, particularly the change of becoming more authentic. I learned to embrace my feelings, to need other people, to let go of controlling, and to depend on God. I learned to own my weaknesses and sinful behaviors, accept my woundedness, and celebrate the positive aspects of who I am. I learned to live in the moment and find joy in little things. And I learned what peace really felt like and what purpose really was. As you read each chapter, I pray you will find words of encouragement and an invitation to embark on this redemptive journey.

Thinking It Over

1. Which of the three legs of your relationship stool are getting attention: Yours? His? Your relationship? Which component do you find yourself focusing on the most? Why?

2. If you haven't taken a step to get help for your "leg," what is holding you back?

3. Have you ever been in training for anything? What did you sacrifice to be able to train for your vision? How did you feel about yourself when you were training?

4. Have you endured other traumatic adversities in your life? How did you grow personally from living through that suffering?

5. If you are willing to accept the challenge, ask God, "What do you want me to learn through the pain of sexual betrayal?" And then keep taking the steps to train in the direction of redemption.

CHAPTER 3

How Could This Have Happened?

Understanding the Real Problem

The roots of all our lives go very, very deep, and we can't really understand a person unless we have the chance of knowing who that person has been, and what that person has done and liked and suffered and believed.

Fred Rogers

Therefore judge nothing before the appointed time; wait till the Lord comes. He will bring to light what is hidden in darkness and will expose the motives of people's hearts.

1 Corinthians 4:5

She yells at him all the time—no wonder he had an affair."

"He never helps with the kids; I can see why she is angry and distant."

"I've noticed that he gazes at women all the time—but if his wife would take care of herself, maybe he wouldn't."

"If he wasn't so angry, maybe his family would want to be around him more."

"He pressures me so much for sex that I just start avoiding him."

"Maybe if I'd just given him more attention, this wouldn't have happened."

Judging symptoms that we can see is easy. Someone is right and someone is wrong. Someone is good and someone is bad. Many of us succumb to this black-and-white thinking. We look at behaviors, survey the symptoms, decide what they mean, and then diagnose the problem. The problem is, if we decide to live this way, we may miss out on the *real* problem. What might be underneath those presenting symptoms? Is a malignant tumor growing somewhere that we can't see?

Christy was a devoted Christian wife and was involved in the music ministry at her church. She was embarrassed to admit in her support group that she had spit at her husband and called him several profane names. She meekly said, "I don't know why I did that. That's not the kind of woman I want to be. Everyone thinks I'm crazy."

Those watching or hearing about the behavior could very easily decide the problem is Christy—maybe she *is* crazy. That's what they see—a raging wife. Someone trying to solve this problem may opt to work with her on simply changing her behavior. All kinds of suggestions could be made: you need to get away until you can calm down; you should call a friend and vent to her instead; you should pray more, read Scripture more, and repent; you need to read some literature about controlling anger. All of these can be helpful ideas, but they only address the tip of the iceberg for Christy. A much bigger story lies beneath the surface. If you really want to know Christy's heart, you need to know her story.

Just two weeks earlier she found pornography on her husband's computer, along with phone bills with numerous out-of-town numbers of women. When she confronted Ryan, he denied any of the phone calls were his and claimed he had quickly glanced at pornography only a couple of times. Christy was devastated and angry. She had always desired a committed, faithful husband. And now she was wondering about their whole ten years of marriage. She expected Ryan to be honest, even if he had done sinful things. She had been honest with him about everything in her life. She had known many men throughout her life who had cheated on their partners—her father, her first boyfriend, and now possibly her own husband. She felt angry and hopeless because she wasn't being heard by her husband. He wouldn't even admit to the obvious facts. Did he think she was stupid? The thought that he might consider her too dumb to figure out what was right in front of her drove her to a place of rage. She was coping with a whole host of feelings, thoughts, and desires. However, she didn't yet have the skills to talk about her story. Her behavior simply mirrored her pain.

Misguided Assumptions

I'm grateful I was led quickly to the deeper issues of sexual betrayal at Family Week and then at my ongoing counseling. If I hadn't been, I would have looked at the behaviors—"Mark has chosen other women instead of me"; I would have surveyed my emotions—"I am brokenhearted, sad, and angry"; I would have judged the behaviors—"If he chooses others, he must not love me"; and I would have made a decision—"I must leave." The verdict would have been black-and-white: "Mark is bad. I am good. There is no hope for our marriage. I deserve better."

We see quick, first-impression diagnoses of sexual sin in our culture every day. We witness infidelity and start making assumptions about the problem and assigning blame. Newspapers are filled with stories of public people and the "falls" they've experienced. We hear the facts about who did what to hurt whom, or who left whom for someone else, but that is about it. We don't hear anything about the story behind the story—the *why* of what happened. The facts lead to assumptions about who was right and who was wrong and to the simplistic comment "That's too bad." These assumptions are full of generalities and judgment. Tragically, they overlook the fact that there is much more truth that needs to be discovered. It is much easier to blame someone or something than it is to seek understanding.

The Wife Is to Blame

When a man chooses to use pornography, have an affair, or act out sexually in any other way, it can be assumed that his sexual desires are not being met in his marriage and he therefore must seek fulfillment elsewhere. Other assumptions about these sexual choices might be that he is under tremendous stress or facing hardship and he needs some kind of release from those demands. There is widespread belief that men *have* to have sex and the wife's duty is to take care of his insatiable sexual needs. There are even books that declare that if a man doesn't have regular sexual release, something bad is going to happen to him! Perhaps another assumption is that infidelity is no big deal because everyone else is doing it. The problem is diagnosed fairly simply: he needs it, he isn't getting it, and so he must find it elsewhere.

Sometimes a wife assumes that she is the problem—that she *caused* this sexual behavior. She automatically blames herself for being a horrible wife. She might assume that she hasn't been available enough—sexually or otherwise—because she has been so tired or preoccupied. Children or work responsibilities may have consumed her days, and now she thinks that if only she had been a better wife, the betrayal probably wouldn't have happened.

Many of these thoughts raced through my mind several hours after the disclosure of Mark's infidelity. He was on the phone doing an intake interview with the treatment center, and I was curled up in a ball sobbing and convincing myself that I hadn't been a very good wife. My energy was depleted trying to raise three active little ones, and I was sure I could never live up to the professional appearances or academic talents of the people with whom Mark spent much of his day. I was confirming in my mind that I wasn't enough, never would be enough, and might as well give up. Until I received wise guidance through the maze of sexual betrayal, the assumption I made was that I caused this sexual acting out. *I* was the problem.

The Husband Is to Blame

Others might assume that *he* is the problem. The one who betrayed you might be labeled as someone consumed with sin, psychologically unbalanced, or broken beyond repair by a bad upbringing or bad choices. "This man who has done some very hurtful things is certainly not the man I fell in love with," you might be thinking. He used to be so caring and kind and wanted to be with you every minute, showering you with affirmations and gifts. What happened to *that* man, you wonder. You think you have done everything a wife is supposed to do, such as being available sexually every time he has asked (which may have been more than you wanted). You've resisted temptation yourself, you've sacrificed your own life in many ways to provide him the time or resources to succeed—and there is no reason he should have betrayed you. *He* is the problem.

Jennifer is convinced that Keith is the problem in their marriage. She confided to me that he had been very sexual before they got married and he was honest in telling her so. "With his horrible upbringing," she said, "I should have known it would always be difficult for him to be sexually pure in our marriage. My family is so opposite from his; they are so kind and encouraging; we never had any problems." In Jennifer's perception, *he* is definitely the problem!

Latisha visited a therapist when she first found out about Damien's affair. She didn't want her family to be split by divorce despite the unfaithful decisions he had made. He hadn't yet admitted that his behaviors were wrong and in fact justified them because he didn't feel loved at home. They had five young children, and Latisha wasn't willing to give up so easily. However, her therapist, who had also met with Damien, bluntly delivered his diagnosis: "He has a narcissistic personality disorder, and he probably will never change." Now it was "professionally" determined that *he* was the problem.

Judith also faced the devastating disclosure that her husband had been looking at pornography for years and had recently been involved with a coworker. He was a successful businessman, who for years hadn't spent much time at home. She managed every aspect of their children's lives and their financial decisions; she sacrificed all of her talents to provide for his career. Although David was remorseful and committed to being sexually pure, Judith repeatedly remarked in counseling sessions that he was just a selfish man—he had always been selfish and that was the problem. If he would figure out how to be unselfish, everything else would be fine. *He* was the problem.

The Culture Is to Blame

Another common conclusion is that the problem is outside *either* of us. We might blame our promiscuous culture: "With women dressing like they do, it's no wonder my husband can't stay sexually pure. He's tempted all the time!" We might think women are much more aggressive these days, that everyone is cheating, that the morals of our country have been lost, or that we would be happier if we would experiment more with sexuality—we might use any number of excuses to justify the sexual betrayal we are facing. Factors *outside* our marriage are the problem.

Gina shared with me that while pornography was detestable to her and she could no longer tolerate it in her marriage, she had actually agreed to watch pornography with her husband in the early months of their marriage. She said she wasn't sure she would like it, but she didn't want to be a prude either; she thought it might help them feel more sexual and playful together, so she agreed to participate. Her husband told her that all couples did this kind of thing and she should loosen up a bit. She decided she was probably quite detached from the "in" fads. Culture was certainly putting pressure on her innocence.

When sexual betrayal is disclosed in a marriage, we are inclined to want to place blame somewhere. Somebody or some condition must be at fault, we think. "Maybe I am the problem. Maybe he is the problem. Maybe we live in a hopeless, sex-infected world and I can't expect anything else." Wherever we put the blame, these perceptions of our marriage and each other lead to division. When sexual sin strikes our relationship, many of these assumptions follow:

- You can't give me what I want anymore; therefore, I need to go somewhere else to get it.
- If we had a good marriage, being connected wouldn't take so much work.
- I've just married the wrong person; you changed after we married; you're not the person I thought I married.
- No other couple struggles the way we do; I deserve to be happy, and since you don't make me happy, I'm entitled to leave.
- If we had better sex, we would have a better marriage.

Whether the problem is seen as yours, his, or the culture's, and whether sexual betrayal is a onetime slip or an addictive pattern, all sexual sin is profoundly wounding to a wife. When husbands are fantasizing or lusting after women, whether it is for real women or images of women, a wife feels compared, objectified, and unchosen. Sexual sin is like a cancer. It has secret cells of pain that, if not found, acknowledged, and treated, will multiply and eventually kill your spirit and your relationship.

Shall We Dance?

All couples, whether suffering from sexual betrayal or not, create "dances" with each other to cope with whatever is going on between them that hasn't been acknowledged and resolved in a healthy way. *All* relationships, in fact, involve such dances, and

knowing how you dance with someone else can be enlighten-
ing. In a relationship, partners develop patterns—routines—of
communication and behavior. For example, when conflict arises,
do you typically run away, or do you try to be a peacemaker and
smooth things over? When someone is hurting, do you feel the
need to fix or to take care of them? Do you get defensive when
you hear something hurtful from a friend or spouse? Do you try
to convince others that your opinions are the best? If you watch
yourself, you will notice patterns that follow you into all of your
relationships. If you tend to avoid conflict, you will do so with
your children, your colleagues, and your friends as well as with
your husband.

What has been important to me while healing from the pain
of sexual betrayal is knowing that *how* I have dealt with that pain
speaks volumes to me about how I react to pain in *all* of my relationships. The pain of betrayal itself was enormous. Learning how
I coped with it, whether I could talk about it, what messages I told
myself about it, and what I was going to do about it said a lot about
how I danced in relationship. Most of the ways I danced in the past
I have decided I didn't like. They hindered my ability to get close
to people and to know myself. I thought the tragedy of sexual betrayal in my life was going to bury me. I had no idea it could lead
me to uncovering the real me and my unique ways of interacting.

Here's a dance Mark and I practiced to perfection in the first
part of our marriage: I saw Mark devoting much of his time to
caring for other women. These women were members of the con-
gregations Mark served, students in classes he taught, clients he
served, or colleagues. I inferred that their needs were more important than mine, and with that assumption I was sad. When I
became sad, I would cope in a couple of ways—I would withdraw
from Mark and decide that I needed to take care of myself and be
independent.

Look at the diagram on the next page to see how the dance
continued. Mark was triggered by the fact that I didn't appear to

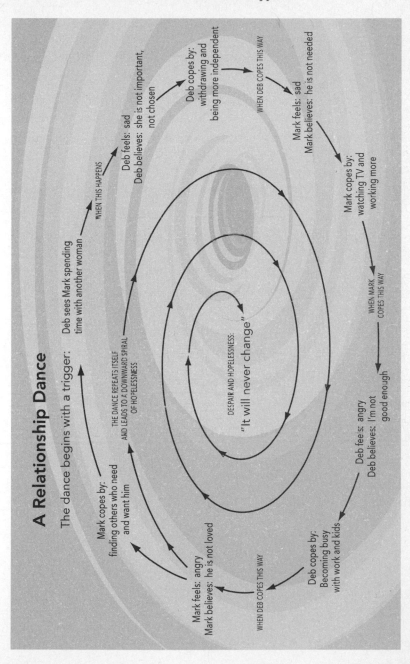

A Relationship Dance

The dance begins with a trigger:

Deb sees Mark spending time with another woman

▶WHEN THIS HAPPENS

Deb feels: sad
Deb believes: she is not important, not chosen

Deb copes by: withdrawing and being more independent

WHEN DEB COPES THIS WAY

Mark feels: sad
Mark believes: he is not needed

Mark copes by: watching TV and working more

WHEN MARK COPES THIS WAY

Deb feels: angry
Deb believes: I'm not good enough

Deb copes by: Becoming busy with work and kids

WHEN DEB COPES THIS WAY

Mark feels: angry
Mark believes: he is not loved

Mark copes by: finding others who need and want him

THE DANCE REPEATS ITSELF AND LEADS TO A DOWNWARD SPIRAL OF HOPELESSNESS

DESPAIR AND HOPELESSNESS:
"It will never change"

need him, and he became sad. He would cope by watching TV or finding more work to do. His behavior then triggered me to think that I wasn't good enough, fun enough, or smart enough to merit his attention, and I would get angry. When I was angry I would get busy with work, the kids, or chores. My busyness in turn triggered Mark. He would get angry that I wasn't available and would cope by finding others who did need or want him. And then we were right back where we started! And so the dance continued until we found a way to talk about what was *really* going on.

Finding a way to talk about my feelings, my assumptions, and my needs didn't happen until I got help. If I had known how to do that, I certainly wouldn't have participated in dances that were killing my spirit!

Here's a pattern Stacy and Brad repeated. Brad would be angry about something and withdraw from Stacy; she would get lonely and afraid of his anger, so she would withdraw as well and comfort herself with eating. He would then feel rejected and angry about her lack of attention and would seek out caring and responsive women on his church committees and talk with them about his loneliness at home (unbeknownst to Stacy). She again would feel hopeless, believing nothing would ever change, and get angry. Then he would get angry that she was angry, and so they would keep on dancing.

Dan and Denise danced this way: Dan spent endless hours at his work. Denise grew resentful of his workload and his inability to help her with their children, so she coped by criticizing him and yelling at the kids. He was angry that he could never do anything right, so he coped by being away even more and turning to pornography for comfort (unbeknownst to Denise). Her resentment grew, and she coped by spending excessive money on clothes and the house to feel better. The debt she incurred led Dan to feel hopeless about providing for his family and resentful that he had no one to help with the financial burden. And so their dance continued.

Helen found her work to be a great place to witness the repetition of her dances. She often complained that she took care of more than her share of family responsibilities. She lived with resentment about the unfairness of life, and she was angry with her husband much of the time. As she observed her work situation, she also noticed that she grew resentful of all of the extra work she continually ended up with. But she didn't know what boundaries to maintain if others demanded she take on more. Helen had been angry for years, but now she was seeing some relational patterns in herself as she struggled with asking for help and stating her frustration and anger when responsibilities became unfair.

Mindy had negative feelings about being sexual when she didn't want to. She was trying to practice being congruent—she wanted to share her honest feelings and fears and not just say yes when her heart was saying no. However, as soon as she saw her husband's agitation and impatience, she talked herself out of what she would say and submitted to his wishes. Afterward she felt sad and hopeless, wanting to give up because things never changed. Her dance with her husband and with others was one of losing her voice midway through the steps. Her feet stopped stepping—her voice stopped speaking her truth.

Can you see how our different dances provide many observable behaviors that we use to inaccurately or incompletely diagnose our real problems? In other words, the problem, or the behavior that we *see*, is only the tip of the iceberg. Beneath the surface lies the expansive foundation of the iceberg, wherein lies a story that will explain the behavior we see. The hidden story holds the rich details of what we have expected, what we have missed, what we have desired, and what we have lost. For most of us, talking about these stories is difficult, and we may not feel safe doing so. Consequently, we figure out ways to cope with the untold story.

The Untold Story

Certain commonalities seem to exist in the stories of men who struggle with sexual sin. If you look into their lives to discover the stories of their growing up, you will hear the pain. To greater and lesser extents, their yearnings to be loved and nurtured, heard and protected, have not been met. Sometimes they have been hurt by people who have physically, verbally, spiritually, or sexually abused them. Sometimes they got the wrong messages about sex from their families, friends, culture, and even church. Sometimes they have just been neglected by people they needed to love them. Whatever happened, their feelings of anger, loneliness, fear, sadness, and anxiety grew, and they didn't have healthy ways to talk about them.

For many men, their sexuality was awakened at an earlier age than was appropriate for a child's development. They may have been touched in sexual ways when young, made to touch others sexually, or exposed to sexual words or pictures at a young age. If their sexuality was awakened as a young child, sexual behaviors became associated with love and nurture — they were intertwined for a child who didn't have the ability to sort out which was which. Sexuality then became a way to find comfort—a way to cope when they were triggered by negative feelings as adults.

Another common thread in some of the men Mark and I work with is that they are very intelligent and creative. We find that they are easily bored and distracted and need a lot of stimulation. Sexual thoughts and activities, especially forbidden ones, become the adrenalin-filled stimulation they crave. Because they didn't get healthy information about sex and because some of them were sexually abused, they grew up with confusion about sexual choices. Most of these men expect marital sexuality to be the answer to their problems. But no woman who has ever lived is capable of providing all that a man needs; thus, sex is the false solution.

Furthermore, many men are angry and disappointed with God because they expected God to fix their problem magically. Anger at God or others always leads to rebellion, and rebellion drives men across their own sexual moral boundaries. Double-mindedness is the result (James 1:8). A part of them wants to be free of sexual sin, but another part desperately wants to hold on to it. If God or their wives aren't going to fix their problem, then they feel angry and entitled to get their needs met elsewhere.

Mark's story is a good example of this dynamic.[1] He was finally able to share with me in our journey of healing that he was sexually abused as a small child. Also, although his mother was a loving provider, she was emotionally and spiritually distant. When he first saw the image of a naked woman smiling at him from the pages of a pornographic magazine, it seemed like the solution to his sadness and loneliness. The ensuing sexual confusion left him without the ability to know the truth. That episode led him into a twenty-five-year history with pornography and masturbation. Those behaviors led him into deeper sexual sin as the pattern escalated. The more he wasn't able to talk about it, the more trapped he became in his silence. By the time we got married, his pattern was already ten years old. He fully expected marital sexuality to cure his sexual sin. The truth is, marital sexuality is not the answer to any person's deep yearning for love and nurture.

I know today that Mark's soul was filled with pain before I even met him. He hadn't taken the time to examine all of the facts of his story (his past), nor did he have skills to talk about it — until he was confronted about his behaviors and encouraged to seek help. Not many of us just sign up for a journey of self-examination. Yet without knowledge of what drives our feelings, thoughts, and decisions, we are left to operate on autopilot — we'll do what looks or feels familiar rather than what is healthy. Mark lived with a lot of loneliness, anger, boredom, and anxiety — in silence. And he eventually chose unhealthy sexual acting out to cope with those feelings.

Sexual addiction or infidelity of any kind is really about searching for something that is missing in one's life—and probably has
been missing for a very long time. It is about using a false substitute for something genuine that is desired. It is an intimacy disorder—a need to connect at a deep emotional and spiritual level
with one's spouse and with others but a lack of the skills to do so.
The problem, then, is much deeper than sexual impurity itself. It
is about a yearning for something more and a determination to
find more—even at emotional, spiritual, and relational prices no
human being can afford.

As a woman wounded by sexual betrayal, you need to know
that you didn't *cause* your husband's sinful choices. With help, you
will learn that you cannot *control* his choices either. If you have
been doing a lot of detective work, setting boundaries for what
he can and cannot do, asking him a lot of questions about his
progress, and deciding what you will do based on how it might
affect his choices for the day, then you are going to need help to
stop controlling. It doesn't work. Unfortunately, most of us don't
know any other way. The surrender of control can create much
fear, resentment, anxiety, and despair.

I can hear you screaming at the page in front of you, "If I don't
do something, then how will things change? I can't just sit back
and do nothing. He'll just think he can do whatever he wants!"
There are things you can say and do that are not controlling, and
we'll talk a lot more about them throughout the rest of this book.

If your husband is diagnosed with sexual addiction or compul-
sion, you also need to know that you cannot *cure* it. You cannot
do the hard work of examining his life and being "good enough"
or compassionate enough to make his sinful behaviors magically
go away. Something is missing that he has been searching for,
and he has chosen other women or sexual acts to fill the void. He
will have to make a decision to examine his life and uncover the
wounds that need healing. Change is possible only if *he* desires to
be a different person.

Unhealthy Coping Strategies Are the Problem

"The problem is never the problem! The way we *cope* with the problem is the problem." These words come from Virginia Satir, a therapist who pioneered theories about family systems in the 1950s, '60s, '70s and '80s. She brought new insights to professionals about how we relate to one another—how in relationship we are hurt and in relationship we heal and grow. If you are in relationship with someone you care about, you will eventually get hurt.

Talking about how we are hurt is very difficult for most of us. Instead of talking about how we feel, we usually find ways to manage or medicate our feelings. Very few of us grew up in families where hurts were discussed; more often, we figure out ways to cope with our feelings by concealing them.

The ways we can choose to cope are endless—and some of those ways can be useful and healthy. Sometimes it is helpful to eat comforting foods, exercise, work on a demanding project, watch a good movie, or curl up with an engaging novel when we feel overwhelmed by difficult emotions. Talking to someone about how we are feeling and what we are choosing to do about it can help relieve our pain and break our isolation. The key is to know *what* choices we are making and *why* we are making them, and to be willing to experiment with coping strategies that are not hurtful to us or others.

Any behavior or substance can be unhealthy. The unhealthy coping strategies Satir is talking about are those that we *habitually* use to cover up, sidestep, or medicate our emotions—usually without any understanding of the motives behind our choices. We might eat junk food when we are angry or sad; we might clean our house obsessively or exercise compulsively or shop till we drop whenever we don't want to experience our feelings. These kinds of coping behaviors always pull us away from intimacy—with others, ourselves, and our Creator. They are only a temporary fix—a

Band-Aid of sorts. The wound is still there; we just figure out how to cover it up for a while, and in the meantime, we disconnect and disengage in a way that is far from conducive to good emotional health.

I loved working when I became frustrated or lonely. With a company to grow, I almost always had something pressing to do. While much of my work was necessary to the welfare of my business, I was constantly looking for even more responsibilities to fill my day. So when I became lonely, I found it easier to charge off to accomplish some task than to try having a vulnerable conversation with Mark about my desire for him to spend more time at home. My work took care of my lonely feelings and became a false substitute for feeling included in my marriage. I had other coping behaviors, too. Busying myself with projects was always a favorite of mine. Overinvolving myself in my kids' lives, volunteering, and withdrawing were other ways I typically coped. These behaviors, when used to medicate loneliness, anger, or any other feeling, never worked to get me what I wanted—more intimacy with Mark. But temporarily, they relieved my feelings and created a sense of peace for me.

If we are to grow and mature, we must be able to identify how we cope. If you're not sure, I encourage you to watch yourself when you have negative feelings: What do you do? How do you act? Your answers will help lead you to your unique coping mechanisms.

Identifying Our Coping Behaviors

All of us have ways of coping, and some are healthier than others. One day in our women's group, we listed all of the ways we personally coped. Look at our list:

☐ Working   ☐ Eating
☐ Reading   ☐ Exercising

- ☐ Volunteering
- ☐ Overinvolving ourselves in our kids' lives
- ☐ Drinking
- ☐ Gambling
- ☐ Isolating ourselves to read the Bible
- ☐ Getting lost in romance novels
- ☐ Engaging in sexual sin
- ☐ Lying
- ☐ Masturbating
- ☐ Withdrawing
- ☐ Raging
- ☐ Sleeping
- ☐ Watching TV
- ☐ Playing video games
- ☐ Taking illegal drugs
- ☐ Taking prescription drugs
- ☐ Daydreaming
- ☐ Shopping
- ☐ Cleaning
- ☐ Playing sports
- ☐ Doing crafts/projects
- ☐ Keeping busy
- ☐ Gardening
- ☐ Engaging in emotional affairs

Perhaps this list includes one or more things that you do on a regular basis. You may not think these behaviors are very important, but your journey of healing involves recognizing that anytime you choose to cope with your feelings instead of being honest about them, you pull yourself away from your relationships. The things you do or use to cope should not be taken lightly.

If you want to heal—to be more emotionally intimate in your relationships—then you must work to understand how you cope and why. Doing so will involve a lot of exploring and processing. Typically, how we cope can be traced back to childhood experiences—either watching those in our family cope in similar ways or being abused in some way that turned us on to this form of coping. We can see definite patterns of coping in families when we look back through the generations.

Did you notice that acting out sexually is on the list? Recognizing this fact is crucial to understanding the real problem you are facing. Acting out sexually is a coping mechanism, just like eating compulsively, raging, watching TV, drinking, reading romance novels, working, and all the rest. But acknowledging that sexual sin is a coping mechanism does not minimize the pain you are experiencing. Sexual acting out is always a sinful choice. Still, you need to understand that it is about coping with feelings such as anger, fear, loneliness, sadness, anxiety, boredom, and disappointment. If you think about one of your coping mechanisms, you'll find that you are medicating one or more of those negative feelings, too. We don't usually need a coping mechanism when we are feeling happy, hopeful, content, or confident. But when we are sad, lonely, tired, angry, or hopeless and we don't know how to talk about those feelings or have safe people with whom to do so, we will usually turn to a coping strategy.

Anika was constantly shopping for new clothes to feel better about herself; she felt insecure as a woman. Kirsten comforted herself daily with wine when her husband yelled at her and criticized the way she did things; she was angry and scared. Zoe busied herself with projects because her husband was never home; she was bored and lonely. Margarita immersed herself in romance novels; she felt rejected and blamed in her marriage.

I want you to hear again: your husband's sexual betrayal is not about you. You didn't cause it. It is one of *his* ways of coping with painful feelings, and it is a horrible, sinful choice. All coping is destructive to those who turn to it. Over time and with repetition, any coping mechanism can become addictive. And whether it is sex or food or work or rage or withdrawal, the consequence of turning toward coping mechanisms instead of safe people and healthy choices is that you will slowly lose your heart—your connection to God and to people you love.

Seeing Clearly beneath the Surface

We all know the story of the *Titanic* and the demise of its glory. The seemingly faultless construction of that gorgeous ship was not enough to keep it from sinking. A hidden iceberg ripped through the side of the ship and destroyed its ability to stay afloat.

Icebergs are similar to us in some ways: just as only their tips can be seen above the water, only a portion of who we are is seen or known by others—and sometimes even by ourselves. And as with an iceberg, much of our beauty and character is hidden. When we go out and greet people throughout our day, they see only what they see: how we are dressed, what we are doing, how we are speaking, and so on. We usually do a good job shining up the part of us that people see—it is our "tip of the iceberg," and we want it to be beautiful. But just as there is much more of an iceberg underwater, so there is much more of who we are: how we are feeling, what expectations we have, what we think or believe about things, how we are struggling, and what we desire. These important parts of our identity are hidden away, however, only to be revealed if we choose to go "underwater" to share them.

We don't often talk about what is "underwater." It is a vulnerable place that most of us haven't learned to access—or if we have, we have been hurt and so we learn to stay "above water." Our hidden iceberg has the capacity to rip us apart, too—and our relationships. It can be a powerfully destructive part of who we are. But it is also the place where we can connect powerfully with other people—underwater, so to speak. Sharing our feelings, perceptions, expectations, yearnings, and truths is the essence of being emotionally intimate with someone. It is what we really seek in our relationships: to know another in this way and to be known.

Virginia Satir created the "personal iceberg metaphor" to explain her theories about relationships. This model is a means by which we can practice congruency in our lives—matching the behaviors people see on the *outside* to the feelings and thoughts we have on the *inside*. If I'm angry because my husband worked late again and didn't call to tell me, I will look and sound angry as well. If I'm sad that I wasn't included in an important gathering, I will look sad and sound sad. Such congruency is the core of authenticity.

Let's look at the layers of Satir's iceberg model. Behaviors that can be observed are at the top of the iceberg. At the very bottom are what Satir calls "I Am" beliefs that reflect a person's deepest sense of self—which her model interprets as basically good.[2]

The Truth about Ourselves

As Christians, we know that God reminds us of the truth about ourselves throughout Scripture. He calls us precious children: "Jesus said, 'Let the little children come to me, and do not hinder them, for the kingdom of heaven belongs to such as these'" (Matt. 19:14). He created us in his image: "I praise you [God] because I am fearfully and wonderfully made" (Ps. 139:14). We are beloved, we are unique, and we are enough: "He created them male and female and blessed them" (Gen. 5:2). "You are a chosen people ... God's special possession" (1 Peter 2:9). These are truths about who we are.

While most of us want to believe these biblical truths, we often internalize very different beliefs. When we have been harmed or neglected in some way as children, we often create new beliefs about ourselves that negate the truths of our faith. Instead of believing that we are special, precious, beloved, and enough, we may believe that we are defective, worthless, unlovable, or never enough. We need to understand how we developed distorted beliefs and how we can reclaim God's truths for ourselves.

What We Desire

If you look at the next layer above "truths," you'll see that we all have what Satir calls "yearnings"—what I call "desires of the heart." According to Satir, all men and women yearn to be loved, accepted, and validated and to have purpose and freedom. Many authors and speakers profess that men have very different yearnings than women do. Books such as *Men Are from Mars, Women Are from Venus* and *His Needs, Her Needs* seek to make us different,

The Iceberg Model

Behaviors

Coping
Unhealthy ways you manage
uncomfortable feelings

Feelings
Joy, anger, hurt, fear, sadness,
anxiety, loneliness, despair

Feelings about Feelings
The decisions you make about your feelings

Perceptions
Beliefs, assumptions, mind-set,
family messages, core beliefs

Expectations
Of self, of others, from others, and of life

Yearnings (Laaser's Seven Desires of the Heart)
To be heard, affirmed, blessed,
safe, touched, chosen, included

Reclaiming the Truth about Ourselves
"Fearfully & wonderfully made," God within

mysterious, and, in many ways, unable to understand each other. Congruent with Satir's model, Mark and I, through our own journey and our work with hundreds of couples, have concluded that men and women have a lot more in common than not. In fact, we have identified seven desires of the heart that we feel are universal to both men and women.[3]

1. *The desire to be heard and understood.* We all long to have someone understand what we are thinking about and feeling. Remember the times in your life when you thought someone wasn't listening or just didn't get it? Were there times in your life when you stopped talking because you didn't think anyone was listening or cared?

2. *The desire to be affirmed.* Affirmation is about something you have done. It is about performance. It is about accomplishment. When you do something well, you long to be noticed and affirmed. Do you find you love being around people who notice the good things you are doing? They encourage you, affirm you, and build you up.

3. *The desire to be blessed.* This desire is about being accepted just for being you—you don't have to *do* anything to be blessed. Affirmation is about what you do; blessing is about who you are.

4. *The desire to be safe.* Safety includes having a safe place to live, food, money, health and medical care, education, and employment. It is about having those basic needs met in order to live in the world without anxiety.

5. *The desire to be touched in healthy, nonsexual ways.* This touch is different from any kind of kissing, petting, genital touch, or otherwise anticipatory touch that leads to sexual intercourse. It is a nurturing touch, a touch to connect without expectation of anything else. It might involve hugging, holding hands, or getting or giving a back rub or a foot or

head massage. This kind of touch says, "I like to be close to you—I need nothing more."

6. *The desire to be chosen.* This desire is about feeling like the "one and only" in someone's life—the cherished one, the soul mate. To be chosen is to know that certain emotions, thoughts, experiences, and conversations are shared only with each other. This desire gets trampled when sexual betrayal enters a marriage. Whether your husband's behavior involves gazing at images of other women, sharing personal information about your relationship, or touching another woman's body, it is hurtful and leaves you feeling "unchosen."

7. *The desire to be included.* Inclusion is the need we have to be part of each other's life as well as part of a safe community of people. We long to belong and don't want to be left out. When we fall in love, we have no problem including each other—in everything. But over time, the practical obligations of life can pull us away from what we yearn to have. We wish to share thoughts, feelings, and activities. We long to know we are needed and that our needs will be attended to. We want to create a vision together. We feel included when others listen to our opinions, respect our ideas, and share information about their lives with us. We have an innate need to belong to a larger community of people who include us in this way. But we also have a desire to be included in our spouse's life in a way that is unique to us.

As Mark and I examined the numerous problems that kept us and other couples stuck, we found that we could always trace a problem "down through the water" to one of the seven desires—and the deep need to have it fulfilled. A thread that runs through the stories we've heard about sexual betrayal is *a yearning for something that is missing.* Knowing the seven desires of the heart can open the door to awareness of what that might be.

Bethany and Pedro fought continually about his work schedule. She complained that he worked too much and that his work
required him to be alone with women too often. Her desire was to
be *included* in his life more and to feel *chosen*. Her expectations were
that if he really chose her and wanted to be with her, he would find
a way to work less and spend more time at home with her. She was
raised in a home where her father was absent most of the week for
his work travels. As a child, she came to believe she was unloved
because her father never spent time with her. She was sad, not
only as a child, but now also as an adult, when loved ones left her
alone. She coped with her sadness by criticizing her husband and
demanding that he leave work. To avoid her anger, Pedro would
figure out ways to stay later at the office.

With help, Bethany and Pedro can now talk about what is going
on for each of them "underwater." As they share their stories, they
can build empathy for each other and learn new ways to meet each
other's desires of the heart.

What We Expect

As we grow up in our families and cultures, we carry the seven
desires into life, and we create *expectations*. We expect that we will
have our desires met. We expect the best from those around us.
But life delivers us both love and harm along the way. Some of us
experience a larger measure of harm, and some of us experience
a larger measure of love. There are no perfect families, churches,
or cultures. We are only human, and humans make mistakes and
have limitations. We can't provide each other with everything we
need. While families, churches, and cultures do the best they can
in most cases, we all leave childhood in some state of incompletion,
having unmet needs and desires.

As children and as adults, we create expectations of ourselves,
of others, and of life. These make up another layer of the iceberg
model. We don't often announce our expectations; we just assume

people will know—that they will be mind readers. Unexpressed expectations can be big or little, and they usually create anger and resentment when they go unfulfilled.

When I married Mark, I had many unspoken expectations for our life together: we would never fight; we would always go to bed at the same time; we would share the responsibilities of the house; Mark would manage our money; Mark's job would be more important than mine (because it was in ministry); we would raise several children; I would stay home with the kids; Mark would be the leader of our home; I would cook healthful meals; TV wouldn't take a high priority—you get the idea. I never talked to Mark about any of these expectations. I figured we were like-minded and the life I envisioned would just happen. In some ways it did, but in many others it did not. Talking about the disappointment when it didn't was difficult to do, and we needed help to get started.

Expectations are often unspoken. We assume our husband knows what we need, and if he doesn't, we assume he must not care. We'll look next at the mistruths we create in our minds.

What We Perceive

The next layer of the iceberg model reflects the perceptions, meanings, and beliefs we derive from our reality. When we see behaviors, we make decisions about what they mean. What we decide may not represent the true reality—it is a mistruth. Generally it is not our nature to check out our perceptions and meanings. We just take them in as fact.

Let's see how this works. Camilla's husband had to travel for business and planned to be away for one week. Camilla was nervous about whether he would be faithful during this time away. She asked if he would call each night to talk to her. Well, Charles did call each night, but on several occasions he told her he was very busy and couldn't talk very long. She called me in a panic, convinced he was meeting another woman and was brushing her off. The *meaning* she made of his rushed phone call was that she wasn't important enough for his time. She *believed* she wasn't loved or good enough for him and assumed he would probably leave. When Charles returned and we could all meet to discuss these perceptions, he apologetically said that a regional boss had arrived at the meeting and requested several extra meetings with him. He was nervous about possible company moves that would affect his job. He didn't take time to explain any of these issues to Camilla because she was short with him on the phone and he worried that she wouldn't hear him out anyway. Her mistruth was that since he didn't have time for her, she was unloved. The real truth was that he did love her but also was distracted by important business.

And so it goes—we create perceptions, meanings, and beliefs about happenings everywhere. You can have some fun with this by becoming a "gentle observer." Just start noticing what you are seeing and what meanings you start attaching to behaviors—yours and others'. We let these meanings start ruling our thoughts and then our decisions without checking out the truth. An important question is "How do we create the perceptions, meanings, and beliefs about behaviors in life?"

Each of us develops a unique "filter" as we grow up, and that filter determines how we see life. Our life experiences are what design our filter. If you grew up in a family that didn't fight, yell, or hit, your filter regarding confrontation is going to be much different than that of someone who lived in the chaos of a verbally and physically abusive home. If you grew up in a single-parent home where money was sparse, your filter regarding self-care is going to be much different than that of someone whose mother stayed at home and whose father was able to privide lavishly for the family. If you grew up in a Christian home, believing God to be a gracious and loving Father, your filter regarding hope and compassion is probably going to be different than that of someone who was blamed, criticized, and thrown out of her home on her eighteenth birthday. Our experiences shape our filters. Our filters determine how we view the world.

Sandra's father was verbally and physically abusive in their home. He was an alcoholic and was very unpredictable—sometimes he was kind and involved with the family; other times he was critical, full of rage, and prone to hit those around him indiscriminately. When Sandra married John, she found that his temper sometimes flared after a long day with an unreasonable boss. He never touched Sandra or criticized her, but his loud voice scared her. Her filter told her to be careful of loud men; that's what she knew from her past. And her unconscious reaction was to withdraw and be quiet. The meaning she made out of John's behavior was that if he was loud, he also might start hitting her. And she told herself she wouldn't be able to do anything about it—she was powerless. (As a child, that would have been true.) As she gained confidence to talk to John about her perceptions, she was able to reframe her truths: he scared her, but he was not out of control; she could ask him to talk differently because she was scared, and he would listen.

Barb, my twin, was very outgoing when we were young, and it was easy for me to be her shadow in many situations. Even our names set up that dynamic for me because *B* came before *D*, and whenever we were called on alphabetically, Barb came first and Deb followed. I didn't identify the trend when I was little, but today I can see that I considered myself to be a follower, not a leader. Not surprisingly, then, I married an outgoing leader. Since my filter tells me my role is to be a shadow, I find it easy to follow Mark in our life together and blend into the background. In many of the things we do together, my perception is that he must lead and I must follow, even though this view is a mistruth about who I am today. Do you see how your past can influence what you believe today?

What you took to be a truth when you were little will continue to affect how you construct truths about your reality today—until you decide to examine the past, reframe the mistruths you carry, and reclaim your truths of today. You'll find it emotionally connecting to keep talking about the perceptions, meanings, or beliefs you're creating from the behaviors you see and whether you believe your interpretations to be truth. Have you ever described your filters to your husband? When both of you share in that kind of "underwater" conversation, you'll discover many new stories about each other. Such conversations allow you to build strong emotional intimacy.

When we have a perception about something or create a meaning or belief about a behavior, they then evoke feelings. If I perceive that Mark is lying to me, I will feel angry. If I have to give a speech but believe I'm inadequate to do so, I might feel nervous or anxious. If you see your husband looking at other women, you will probably feel sad or angry. All perceptions, meanings, and beliefs lead us to the next level—feelings, and the feelings we have about our feelings.

What We Feel

The next two layers of the iceberg model include our feelings and the feelings we have about those feelings. We are full of feelings—all of us. They are an extremely rich part of who we are! Feelings are stored in the heart. Proverbs 4:23 tells us, "Above all else, guard your heart for everything you do flows from it." Our senior pastor gave an excellent sermon on this passage. He talked about the vital signs of a healthy heart: you feel deep emotions; you can live in the moment; you have room for fun, spontaneity, and laughter; you have compassion for the needy and lost; you can quiet your heart enough to hear God's whisper.

Do you allow deep emotions to flow through your heart? Living in the moment encourages a whole range of emotions: joy, disappointment, anger, impatience, excitement, anxiety, loneliness, and more. Do you know what it feels like to give expression to each of those emotions? Feelings are the foundation to building emotional intimacy. If you can't talk about your feelings, you can't get "underwater." And it's underwater where we find the rich stories of our lives and the connection to others—the wellspring of life.

Unfortunately, many of us have been taught to hide our feelings and experience them alone—at least the "negative" ones. We may be comfortable sharing our joy, hope, excitement, contentment, or other positive feelings, but we think we need to do away with those other ones. Maybe you've been taught to look for the good in everything (and ignore the bad); maybe you've learned that Christians shouldn't worry or be sad; or maybe you believe anger isn't very feminine or attractive. Perhaps you've never seen anyone cry in your family, especially men. Feelings can be so uncomfortable that we are taught to minimize them, deny them, or avoid them. It's easier to talk about "above-water" kinds of things—such as what you or others are *doing* or *accomplishing.*

How familiar are you with what you are honestly feeling? Do you use words other than *fine, good, tired,* or *okay* to describe how you are feeling? Here's a list of a broad spectrum of specific feelings:

☐ Glad	☐ Hopeful
☐ Sad	☐ Prideful
☐ Angry	☐ Frustrated
☐ Afraid	☐ Exhausted
☐ Lonely	☐ Embarrassed
☐ Anxious	☐ Happy
☐ Hurt	☐ Eager
☐ Guilty	☐ Cautious
☐ Joyful	☐ Shocked
☐ Nervous	☐ Confident
☐ Depressed	☐ Disappointed
☐ Bored	☐ Grateful
☐ Overwhelmed	☐ Surprised
☐ Ashamed	☐ Confused
☐ Jealous	☐ Hopeless
☐ Hysterical	☐ Conflicted

Do you use any of these words in conversation? Try inserting some of these feeling words into your next conversation and see how you do. For example:

I feel *conflicted* today about what I need to do and what I want to do.

I feel *hopeless* about our marriage.

I feel *anxious* about providing for myself if we don't make it through this crisis.

I am *sad* and *angry* that you won't stop looking at pornography.

Many experts declare that women are more in touch with their emotions than men, so I find it fascinating when women first come to group and are asked to check in with their feelings. They often have no idea what to say! Here are some common responses: "I don't really know what I'm feeling today." Or, "I have such a hard time coming up with a word to describe what I'm feeling." Or, "I hate this part. [*Chuckle.*] I've been thinking about what to say ever since I left the house this morning." In other words, women struggle to talk about their feelings just as men do. In fact, instead of stating our feelings about a situation, we often turn them into a question. Rather than saying directly, "I feel sad and angry that you won't stop looking at pornography," we might communicate our feelings indirectly: "Don't you think it's important to stop looking at pornography?" Or instead of saying, "I feel conflicted today about what I need to do and what I want to do," we might ask, "Do you think I should stay home with Chloe or go to my group?" I find that women aren't as accomplished at talking about their emotions as they are at interrogating!

Observe yourself for a while and evaluate your expression of your feelings—*gently.* If you find that you talk mostly about facts and behaviors (which most of us do), then everything becomes black and white, right or wrong, good or bad. Those listening to you will probably become defensive because they feel attacked.

Consider these examples:

I found ten receipts for videos that you hid from me.	*That is wrong!*
I've seen you gazing at women when we go to restaurants.	*You are bad!*
You need to promise never to lie again, or I'm leaving.	*You must be perfect.*

Black-and-white conversations divide us and frustrate us and keep us from experiencing real intimacy—knowing another person's heart and being known. Feelings are the building blocks of deeper conversations. They lead us into a world of gray, where we ponder perceptions and possibilities. Feelings are not right or wrong, good or bad—they just *are*. Feelings drive our lives—they are the gasoline that makes us go. We can decide where we want to go, or we can move along on autopilot; the choice is up to us. When we know how to talk about our feelings, then we can be *intentional* about what we will do in relation to them.

The "feelings about feelings" layer describes the decisions we make about the feelings we have. I remember telling my therapist that I was sick and tired of being sad; I asked her if these feelings would ever end. Then somewhere in my mind I decided that I had been sad long enough and it was time to move on! You might be angry because you still feel frustrated, or afraid because you feel hopeless, or anxious because you can't stop feeling anxious. We can experience many feelings about the feelings we have.

Our feelings eventually lead us to choices about what we will do—or how we will *cope* with those feelings. If you don't have much experience naming your feelings and talking about them, or you don't feel safe sharing them, you will find a way to cope with them. When you are coping, the feelings you have begin to subside—the substitute feels good. This pattern of feeling something, avoiding the feeling, and then substituting a behavior or substance to feel better becomes an unconscious cycle of coping—you're on auto pilot and are unavailable for the intimacy your heart yearns for.

Our Common Suffering

Our adaptation of Virginia Satir's model is intended to help you dig deeper into your life and grow in character. It can help you to have more authentic conversations with others and develop greater self-awareness. It can give you hope that change is always possible. Each of us needs to be reminded that *my* coping is about making a choice to deal with *my* pain and *my* unmet desires; it is not about someone else. This concept is a hard one to accept. We are all narcissistic in that we tend to make others' choices about ourselves!

All of us long to have the desires of our hearts met. Each of us has been disappointed throughout our growing-up years that our family, church, and culture couldn't fulfill the desires of our aching hearts. And then we found the love of our life, our soul mate. We thought our desires would be fulfilled at last, only to experience the ache of disappointment that our marriage partner couldn't always fulfill our wishes. Our unmet desires led to unspoken expectations and to perceptions about behaviors; our perceptions created feelings that required medicating or coping. Our coping often led us to blame each other and distance ourselves and assume that our partner's coping was about us.

So our challenge becomes accepting that we *all* suffer in some way—we all carry secret pain deep within our hearts. We can choose to know about each other's pain and to be companions in growing our character through adversity. Moreover, by acknowledging that only God can truly fulfill the desires of our hearts, we'll see that we expect far too much of each other at times.

In *Sacred Marriage*, Gary Thomas relates profound insights about marriage as a place where God can transform us from the inside out. He says, "We want to get the largest portion of our life's fulfillment from our relationship with our spouse. That's asking too much. Yes, without a doubt there should be moments of happiness, meaning, and a general sense of fulfillment. But my wife [husband] cannot be God, and I was created with a spirit that craves God. Anything less than God and I'll feel an ache."[4]

When we turn to God to understand our aches and trust that he will fulfill the desires of our heart, we can then be more content with what we do receive from our husband and others.

Thinking It Over

1. Whom have you wanted to blame for your husband's sexual betrayal?

2. Which of the seven desires were met when you were growing up? Which do you still yearn for today?

3. When you feel angry, lonely, tired, bored, anxious, or hopeless, how do you cope?

4. Are you willing to share the stories of your pain with your husband and to hear his? Why or why not?

CHAPTER 4

Where Can I Hide My Heart?

The Journey through Brokenness

Were it possible for us to see further than our knowledge reaches, perhaps we would endure our sadnesses with greater confidence than our joys. For they are moments when something new has entered into us, something unknown.

Rainer Maria Rilke

The LORD is close to the brokenhearted and saves those who are crushed in spirit.

Psalm 34:18

When I walked down the red-carpeted aisle of my mother and father-in-law's church to be married to their son, I thought I had stepped into a fairyland. The church was overflowing with guests—people who had watched Mark and me fall in love and commit to a life of "happily ever after." I had created many expectations of the life we would live and the husband I was marrying. Mark and I had been dating for four years before we were married, but most of that time was spent apart from each other on different college campuses. We craved being together—Mark drove his little Volkswagen Bug from Rock Island, Illinois, almost every weekend to see me at Iowa State, a three-and-a-half-hour drive at 80 mph (that was legal in the seventies!). When we weren't together, we were racking up huge phone bills talking from our dorm rooms, longing for the day we could finally be married. We wrote letters to each other, composed poems, made gifts, bought flowers—my dreams of the future were shaped by these passionate days together.

I had a fantasy of the husband I was marrying: he would be a gifted spiritual man, a great leader of our home, a passionate lover, a sensitive and gentle husband, an athlete, an intellectual, a playful spouse, a listening and engaged father. He would be good-looking, attentive to my needs, encouraging, available—a man who would always take care of the children and me and lead us to be a godly family. He would be my prince! I had no doubt he was going to be all of those things. All I had to do was say, "I do!" and this wonderful reality would begin.

For most of my marriage, I thought I was living the storybook life. I could easily displace my feelings of loneliness or sadness with the joys of a lovely home, three spirited children, and a husband meaningfully engaged in our lives and his work. Although my husband wasn't always the prince I had dreamed about, I silenced my disappointments or frustrations by keeping busy or being quiet. I didn't know how to deal with those tugs at my heart that tried to warn me that Mark seemed overly busy with others and less and less interested in me. There was so much about ministry that he was "called" to do, and I couldn't expect his time or attention when others needed it. I learned to hush those dreams of long ago and turn to my own work, the kids, and friends for companionship if I was lonely. And then when we did experience times when our family connected or Mark and I shared about our work, I told myself I just wasn't grateful enough for what I had. The ache in my heart led me to wonder if something was missing, but my intellect told me I was crazy—it didn't get much better than this. My "spiritual" side told me I shouldn't interfere with God's call on my husband's life and that I should sacrifice any needs or desires I had.

While my fantasy husband and dream life weren't perfect, they were close. But then the disclosure of sexual betrayal shattered everything. Sexual fidelity was a promise we made, a vow we took before God and those we loved. It stood at the core of our choosing each other, solely and completely. Giving myself sexually to my husband was the most intimate thing I had ever done. I had never shared my body with anyone else. It was saved for him — only him. It was the sacred gift I gave to him to symbolize the deepest connection I was ever to make with another human being. "The two shall become one" — and I thought we were truly one. I thought I was being cherished for sharing this sacred gift just as I was cherishing him. I desired to have his eyes only ever choose me; I wanted to know I would always be enough and that he would always be content with who I was.

So what was I to make of this new information? If Mark had been sexual with other women or even had strictly emotional connections with other women, then I assumed I was unchosen. My husband went elsewhere to have his needs met; thus, I must have fallen short in some way. Furthermore, since he also hid his behaviors and lied about them, I didn't know whether anything in our marriage was real. The lies were almost worse than his actions, leading me to think I must not have been the friend and soul mate I thought I was. The foundation of my marriage was crumbling. The memories of my life with Mark were disintegrating. I wanted to shout out to someone who would listen, "Is anything about my life real? Is it all a farce? Am I such a horrible wife that my husband had to go to other women? Surely something must be wrong with me."

My life seemed to lie in ruins, and my mind raced with a million thoughts. "God, why would you allow this horrible thing to happen to me? Where are you anyway? Can't you see I'm trying hard to be a good wife and mother? Don't you care about me? Have I wasted all of these years thinking we had a good marriage? I'm not sure I even know the man I married!" My dream of "happily ever after" was shattered. I couldn't imagine feeling loved again — or loving Mark again.

Naming Your Losses

Sexual betrayal can deliver a whole host of losses. It is important for you to grieve these emotional and tangible losses—to grieve the life that has been torn apart and the lost dreams you held for your marriage.

The loss I felt immediately after disclosure was that of trust. Mark was the man in whom I had placed my total, unquestioning trust. I never even thought of him as being anything but trustworthy. If I had a twinge of suspicion about his whereabouts, his choices, or his behaviors, I talked myself out of it or minimized my doubts about his credibility. If anything was to be questioned, it was my mind for thinking anything but the best of my husband. I had placed Mark on a very high pedestal, and now he'd come tumbling down. I knew living with someone I wasn't sure I could trust again was going to be difficult.

A major loss for Mark, and thus the whole family, was his job as a pastoral counselor. His colleagues granted him one month's compensation and sent him on his way. Furthermore, his treatment counselors advised him not to work for one year after leaving treatment. So while he was there, he was directed to call and resign from the two other part-time positions he held. By the end of his first month in treatment, all employment was gone. These employment losses were crushing consequences for Mark, but they were my losses, too.

Women may also face financial losses if products or services have been purchased as part of their husband's sexual acting out. Some men have spent thousands of dollars for pornography, massages, strip clubs, prostitutes, hotels, gifts, and travel to meet up with affair partners. For many couples, these expenses put a tremendous strain on the family budget. Tragically, some women don't even know that money has been siphoned from the family.

Health losses can be a consequence of sexual sin. If there has been unprotected sex outside of your marriage, you may have contracted a sexually transmitted disease or even HIV/AIDS. There is expense and embarrassment of testing, another loss of dignity and finances. And even if there was not sexual contact with another person, either of you may have been experiencing health issues as a result of stress or unconscious suffering.

Currently I'm counseling a woman who has chronic stomach-aches and intestinal infections. Heidi has been treated for several months, and doctors still can't accurately diagnose her symptoms. When I asked her if her husband had told her about all of his acting out, she said she didn't think so. "When I ask, he just shuts down and won't talk," she explained. In the meantime, she has seen doctors many times, is taking long-term antibiotics, and still has pain. She is beginning to trust her intuition that the antibiotics are masking the physical results of the STD tests she took and that her husband is still lying to cover up sexual contact he has had.

My TIA, the transient ischemic attack that temporarily paralyzed my right side, has continued to cost me a great deal in insurance costs. With that diagnosis on my chart, I was unable to get disability insurance. My health insurance was available at a premium cost, and the cost of life insurance also was much higher for ten years.

The loss of reputation or respect in the community faces some couples. Sexual sin almost always creates gossip and judgment when people find out. Depending on the nature of the sexual betrayal, you may feel people withdrawing from you and even denying you opportunities to serve on committees, work at certain jobs, or be included in some groups. Judgment and criticism often come from those who don't have a clear understanding of sexual sin.

When Mark's sexual sin was reported in our area newspapers, he was ostracized by many people. Even the leaders of the church in which he was ordained refused to talk to him. And even though it was *Mark's* behavior that was being reported, I carried the shame of his actions and felt my own sense of loss of reputation. I remember going to the store and not wanting to sign my check for fear that the clerk would recognize my last name. I was definitely hiding from the public and any judgment I thought they would have of Mark or me.

A loss of freedom occurs once sexual sin has entered your relationship. Now you must make decisions about what you will say and to whom you will share information. Depending on the nature of the sexual betrayal, you may need to be very careful about who finds out—employers, teachers, friends, and family.

You may lose your home and need to move because of your husband's sexual acting out. If a job change is necessary, you might not be able to find work in the same city. If financial issues have stressed your budget, you may need to move to a smaller residence. If coping with the pain requires you and your husband to live separately, one of you will need to move out and incur many extra expenses.

Catherine's husband had had a longtime affair with a next-door neighbor. To heal as a couple and not be triggered by memories of that relationship, they decided to sell their house and move to a new community. Cindy's husband had had numerous affairs, and one of the women with whom he'd been involved bought the house across the street from Cindy and her husband. Although involved in recovery, Cindy and her husband decided to move again to start fresh.

Mark and I made a decision to move to a new city eighteen months after his disclosure. Given the publicity of Mark's case, he would have had difficulty finding professional work in his field. With that move, our children lost friends and faced the challenges of starting over at new schools. I also left great friends and was faced with the additional need to relocate my company.

We certainly lose our dreams of happily ever after and our fantasies of Prince Charming. We lose the barometer for gauging happiness and contentment. For some of us, happiness might have been a calm lifestyle or problem-free kids or passionate sex or enough money to be worry-free. With new information about sexual sin, we are forced to think about how we will measure our joy.

The tangible losses are easier to identify and assess. But many intangible, emotional losses occur, too. The peace that you may have been working hard to attain for your family is now replaced with anxiety; contentment is seemingly lost forever, giving way to anger, sadness, and fear. The confidence you may have had in your family unit will change to confusion, innocence to suspicion, trust to mistrust, and hopefulness to hopelessness. The emotional toll is smothering and paralyzing at times. Acknowledging these emotional losses is crucial to your healing.

It is important to name your losses, both physical and emotional. Facing the reality of your life is an important first step to healing. You are promised that "the truth will set you free" (John 8:32); first you must be willing to identify the truth about your losses.

A Time to Grieve

In the ancient words of a wise king, "There is a time for everything, and a season for every activity under the heavens: … a time to tear down and a time to build, … a time to weep and a time to laugh, a time to mourn and a time to dance" (Eccles. 3:1, 3–4).

After the disclosure of Mark's sexual betrayal, it was time for tearing down, for weeping and for mourning losses. I couldn't fathom building, laughing, or dancing. Sexual sin caused many losses in my life. They were real losses, and they created real consequences for both of us. You have experienced losses, too. If you haven't stopped to look at what you have lost and to account for the expenses of sexual sin, you may not even know why you have so much to grieve.

Do you know how to grieve? I certainly didn't. I knew I was sad a lot. Tears flowed at the most unexpected times. I lost interest in almost everything. I moved through my days with my to-do list

directing me around. One day I visited my therapist and told her
I thought I might be getting clinically depressed; I didn't know
what was happening to me. After talking about many of the losses
in my life, she wondered aloud with me if I was just grieving. The
diagnosis seemed to fit for me. I realized I wasn't only grieving the
losses resulting from Mark's sexual acting out, but also facing many
changes in my life because of consequences. All of these changes
created loss, and all loss requires grieving. I was relieved to be able
to name this process and to know that I needed to embrace it so I
could heal.

In *How People Grow*, Drs. Henry Cloud and John Townsend
describe grief this way:

> Grief is the toughest pain we have to deal with. It is not the
> worst human experience, because it leads to resolution, but
> it is the most difficult for us to enter into voluntarily, which
> is the only way to get into it. The rest of our human experi-
> ence just happens "to us." Hurt, injury, anxiety, alienation and
> failure all break through, and we suffer. Grief does not "break
> through." It is something we enter into.... Grief is God's way
> of our getting finished with the bad stuff of life. It is the pro-
> cess by which we "get over it," by which we "let it go." ... The
> soul is designed to finish things. It is designed to grieve. Just as
> a computer is programmed to run a particular path, so our soul
> is designed to go down the path of grief. Therefore, since it is
> the way we are made, Solomon tells us, basically, to "get on
> with the program." Be sad, and your heart can be made happy.
> Cry it out, and it will get out. It will be over.[1]

Grieving is the process of emotions we experience in reaction
to a loss.[2] Many helpful books deal with the stages of grief: for
example, *Good Grief* by Granger Westberg, *On Death and Dying*
by Elizabeth Kubler-Ross, *Living with Dying* by Glen W. David-
son, and *How People Grow* by Cloud and Townsend. I've found it
beneficial to think about *elements* of grieving rather than stages. I

personally experienced many different emotions that seemed all mixed up at times—repeating themselves or even disappearing for a while, only to reappear at another place or time. Grieving was not a well-ordered process with a well-defined beginning and end.

A Time to Be Numb

The first element of grieving has to do with experiencing a bad situation—with being shocked and numb about the loss of what you thought you had. You live in disbelief that this crisis could be happening to you. Although Jesus reminded us that "in this world [we] will have trouble" (John 16:33), most of us still go about our lives believing these bad things surely won't happen to us. Some might think that because they are careful, smart, or in control, they can avoid the adversity that others face. Thus, when something horrible does happen, they are shocked and numb.

Victoria was confronted by several police officers at her front door, informing her that her husband had been detained for carrying pictures of naked minors in his suitcase while traveling. They were at her home to confiscate computers or any other evidence they could find. For over an hour they searched her home while she sat with an officer in her living room. She reported several weeks later that she just didn't feel anything anymore. She wasn't crying; she wasn't angry; she just went about her life as if she were floating through her days. And she couldn't figure it out. "Is something wrong with me?" she asked. Nothing was wrong with her—she was simply experiencing the numbness that often follows a terrible shock.

A Time to Deny

Denial is another element of grieving. It's like having a bad dream and thinking you'll surely wake up soon. You don't want to believe your life has been affected this way, so you start to believe the situation isn't so bad. In my case, I was angry with everyone around Mark, wanting to justify some of the horrible truths about his behavior by blaming them. If women hadn't been so needy or dressed so provocatively, if colleagues had been more helpful, or if we hadn't been under such financial stress all the time, surely he wouldn't have made these sinful choices. I didn't want to believe that the situation was about my husband. I needed it to be about someone or something else.

A Time to Bargain

Grieving may involve bargaining, which has to do with a desperate yearning to improve the situation or lessen the pain. "Maybe if I don't talk to anyone about this sexual infidelity that is ruining my life, it won't seem so bad." Or, "If we could just move to another city, I wouldn't have to be reminded of the places I know my husband has been." We bargain away, if not literally, then at least in our minds, to make things seem better. The wish remains that somehow, some way, something must work to ease the suffering and humiliation of sexual betrayal.

A Time to Be Angry

After your dreams have been shattered, you may experience a time of intense anger. Anger is another component of grieving. Something you expected to have—commitment to your marriage vows—has been lost. You exchanged those precious words at the altar with the full expectation that they would be honored, but now the rings you wear to symbolize that sacred day seem meaningless. Even looking at them is difficult. "What meaning do they hold now?" you wonder. Years of faithfulness seem wasted. "I'll never get those years back," you might be saying. You might even be thinking, "I don't even know who my husband is anymore. He certainly isn't the man I married."

I had a very hard time being angry with Mark in the beginning. He was so broken and remorseful for what he had done that I couldn't imagine rubbing salt in the wound. I found it much easier to be angry with the women who must have "chased after him," the church that ignored him, the colleagues who seemed so callous, the attorneys who didn't seem aggressive enough—anyone and everyone except Mark. I found it easier simply to be sad for him and for me.

But a lot of women in my groups are out of control with their anger, verbally abusing and sometimes even physically abusing their husbands because they can't stop venting their disgust and disappointment. Nancy, for example, demanded her husband sleep on the couch downstairs after she found out about his affairs. She was so angry that she had kicked in the front dash of the car when they were trying to have a conversation one day. And one night, after he had fallen asleep, she came downstairs and began hitting him because she was so full of rage.

Sometimes the anger we hold inside spills out on others we love, especially children. We may be very short-tempered or critical or demanding without just cause. Or we may be extremely sarcastic or belittling to get back for the hurt inflicted on us. Terri confessed week after week in her women's group that she couldn't control her tongue—she was always finding ways to make cutting remarks to her husband, who had decided to leave her for another woman. Some of us, rather than venting our anger, just hold it in. The suppression of anger leads to other consequences, including physical symptoms such as headaches, stomachaches, backaches, and a host of other illnesses. We may start to feel like a runaway roller coaster, emotionally out of control. Or we may just drop into depression as a way to avoid the whole ordeal.

If you don't choose to deal with your anger in a healthy way, you will stay stuck and feel like a victim. A victim is someone who feels she has no choices, whose life is determined by what others do to her. Being a victim is a horribly powerless place to be. It's like sitting in the middle of a road watching a tornado move toward you and not being able to get out of the way, to hide, or to stop the storm. Carrying anger around unchecked and unresolved will destroy you and those around you and will sabotage any effort to restore relationships or make healthy choices for yourself.

Terri's husband did proceed to divorce her, making outrageous requests and stating many mistruths about her in the court proceedings. She worked diligently to express her anger in group and to grieve the losses of her heartbreaking situation. She learned to stay grounded in the truth that she was a good person and a good mother when facing endless interrogation. She was also willing to own the things she had done to create a hostile environment. She had safe women accompany her to difficult court appearances to support her. She practiced acknowledging her feelings and needs and not blaming her husband—characteristics that were vital to becoming the woman she wanted to be even after divorce. She was transforming her life, even in the midst of a very painful, very expensive end to her marriage.

The first step in dealing with your anger is to be "heard" by someone about it. I was fortunate to have several places where I could be heard about my anger. Since Mark was so broken about his sexual acting out, he was willing to hear my cries of injustice and hate and confusion when I was finally able to voice those feelings. As I mentioned earlier, I needed help even to access those feelings with authentic words, tones, and behaviors because I was shut down from expressing anger in a congruent way. I wanted to look and sound like a "nice girl" and a "good Christian woman," so simply letting my anger fly wasn't acceptable to me. Fortunately, I had the safety of my women's group in which to experiment with the out-of-control anger that was soon to come. I learned that when someone like me has bottled up anger for so long and then begins to let it out, it comes blasting out! The enormity of my pain would have been overwhelming if I had let only Mark hear it. My purpose in expressing anger and pain was to move forward, to find healing—not to destroy my relationship with Mark. I'm grateful I was directed to other safe women who could support me in that process.

I see many women stuck at this point, often because their husband doesn't seem particularly remorseful about his sexual sin. He may not own how hurtful it has been to her; in fact, he really may not be broken about it at all. Even though he may have decided he needs to get help for his problem and may encourage his wife to stay and work through this difficult time, he fails to show obvious remorse or adequate acknowledgment of the damage he has done. Wives who live in such a situation struggle with being heard and often can't understand why they stay stuck blaming him for past behaviors (and probably current ones, too) or attempting to get revenge.

If I have just described your situation, I urge you to think about a therapist or other safe women as people who can hear you and your feelings. Your husband isn't the only one who can validate your reality. In fact, the one who betrayed you may *never* be able or willing to hear your heart or make amends for what he has done. Nevertheless, your emotional and physical health is worth your being heard and getting unstuck.

Other ways to work on your anger include journaling or writing letters to those who have harmed you (letters *not* usually sent, by the way). Allowing the raw emotions of anger that you are feeling to find expression in words is a wonderful way to disempower them. Anytime you take something inside of you—an emotion—and find a way to give it outward expression, you'll feel a sense of relief. Try it out for yourself and notice what happens. So often we let emotions fester in our body and grow like cancer cells. We need to get them out.

Another helpful way to work on anger is to do something physical to represent removing the emotion from your heart. The

practice may not be so prevalent today, but my therapist encouraged us to hit pillows with a racquet while speaking truths about
our anger. We did our swinging in group to experience further
validation of our truths. I still have a hard time picturing myself
doing that! But swing away I did, yelling at the judge who bought
our lovely home while we suffered with lawsuits that were potentially destroying the stability of our family. "You may take my
home," I screamed, "but you won't take my soul!" And on and on
I went. I'll never forget that night at group; I am forever grateful
to know that I can rid myself of toxic anger.

A Time to Be Sad

Many wives I've talked with simply don't know how to move from
anger to the sadness that lies underneath. When they were growing up, they didn't see others being unhappy or sad, and they were
discouraged from having such emotions themselves—"It's going
to be okay; get over it." Or, "If you don't stop crying, I'll give you
something to cry about!" They may have received many messages
that shut down normal, healthy expressions of sadness. On the
other hand, you may have seen anger all the time—venomous
words exchanged between family members, critical comments
meant to put others in their place, blaming statements intended to
show who was in charge, or sarcasm (a very subtle way of expressing anger by covering it with humor). I don't know what you witnessed in terms of anger and sadness, but I do know it affects how
you will deal with those feelings in your relationship now.

Sara was a social worker and a soft-spoken woman. She was furious with her husband, who had been fired from his pastoral position after having several affairs. They were separated and working
diligently on their personal development. Sara's friend Pam knew
she needed to let go of her enormous angry energy—it was killing her spirit. So Pam went to several garage sales and bought all
of the cheap dishes she could find. Then she found an old empty

warehouse whose owner gave her permission to borrow the facility for a day. Pam took Sara there and unloaded the pile of dishes. She instructed Sara to start throwing them, one by one, and yelling out her resentments and losses as she did. Unspeakable words were flying as dishes were crashing—and slowly, slowly, Sara's aching heart spit out the poison of her anger. When she was finished, she accepted the embrace of her dear friend and "validator" as she accessed her deeply saddened soul.

Julie lived with continual criticism from both her mom and dad when growing up. Yelling was par for the course in her family of five children. No one was allowed to show a sad face—ever—or they would pay for it. Physical punishment was common; the sharing of real emotions was not. Julie remained angry for most of the first year she participated in her women's group. Anger was her normal response to all hurt and pain. And then a switch happened for her—she found her tears. With the support and encouragement of other women, she began to let losses in her life emerge with accompanying sadness. And she was validated for being real—authentic. She stayed in that congruent place for many months and sent me an email one day: "I think last year was my year to be angry, and now this one is my year to be sad. I feel like I'm making great progress!"

Julie did make great progress, and interestingly, her husband began "hearing" her pain as well. When her anger moved to the losses and sadness she felt, he was able to stay present to validate her pain without getting defensive. It was a victory for their relationship as well as for her personal growth.

While we need to experience our anger and voice it, we also need to know how to express sadness so that we'll get what we really need—to be heard. Some women complain that their husband just doesn't get it. He doesn't understand how much pain he has caused his wife. Yet when I question some wives about whether they are sharing their sadness with their husband, I often get a subdued "No, not really. I usually cry by myself. He isn't very comfortable when I'm sad." I'm amazed that so many women say the same thing. You can imagine I jump all over those kinds of statements! If you want to be heard, you must be honest about your feelings, regardless of the way your husband handles it. He can't validate your pain if it only shows up as anger; you must show him the authentic pain of your broken heart.

Barbara was a beautiful professional woman who worked for a Christian organization. She was raised in a legalistic Christian home, the daughter of a pastor. Sadness wasn't acceptable in her home. She needed to be grateful for whatever was happening; if she was sad, she was told that she wasn't looking for the goodness of the Lord. But she cried a lot about her husband's unfaithfulness and her desire for him to understand the hurt his behavior had caused her. In fact, she was so in touch with her emotions when we talked together that it never occurred to me that her husband might not have seen those tears. But when I thought to ask her if she sounded and looked this way when she spoke to him, she said she never did. She was only angry with him. Her sadness was saved for times alone — "safe" times when she wouldn't be scolded or talked out of her feelings as she always had been when she was growing up.

Grieving involves despair and sadness as you accept that the loss you are dealing with is all too real. It has impacted your life profoundly, and it is not going away. You feel hopeless, out of control. You feel as though you are at the bottom, and your tears won't stop. This is the time when many women give up trying to heal or to find purpose in this adversity because it is too hard to feel the pain — to say good-bye to what has been lost and to really let go. Some women have never been allowed to show sorrow and simply don't know how to embrace feelings of despair; some think crying is a sign of weakness; others talk themselves out of staying in the relationship during this stage because they feel they have been sad too long and don't want to look pitiful or self-absorbed. Some just choose to find a new relationship and start over.

A Time to Be Depressed

Many women who have been through the trauma of sexual betrayal experience crippling depression. I don't have any academic degree to warrant my giving advice of any kind on this subject. However, I do know that feelings of depression can be frightening and overwhelming. They can consume your thoughts, kill all desire to enjoy life, or paralyze you from managing your daily responsibilities. They can be so out of control that you can't stop crying, can't stop raging, can't stop isolating yourself or feeling crazy. In some cases, the emotions triggered by shattered dreams can make you feel desperate to end your misery—even at the cost of ending your life. There are times when you need medical advice and perhaps medication to help you through clinical depression.

Drs. Archibald Hart and Catherine Hart Weber, in their book *Unveiling Depression in Women*, share some very helpful information for understanding what depression is, who gets it, what causes it, and how it can be treated. They explain depression this way:

> Any meaningful loss has the potential to trigger depression. In general, the more meaningful the loss, the greater the depression.... Somewhere in all the pain of depression, there has to be a message. Even when depression seems to come out of nowhere, it starts with a part of you signaling that something is not quite right. At the very least, it's a way of getting you to stop and think about your life—and possibly make some changes. It's all part of our human existence and God's alert system for our bodies, minds, emotions, and relationships, and we would be wise to heed these signals and warnings. It helps, therefore, to pause and ask yourself: "What is my depression telling me?"[3]

Suzanne had suffered from depression most of her marriage. She said she was diagnosed and given medication by her family practice physician after one year of marriage. She had gone in for

an annual exam and reported her symptoms of lethargy, sleepless-
ness, and fear of being married. She was told she probably was
reacting to the transition in her life and was given medication to
help her make that change.

Five years later, she found out that her husband was looking at
pornography and connecting regularly with women online. They
found help to heal their marriage of the sexual betrayal, and in
doing so, Suzanne began revisiting incidents in her life of early
sexual abuse. She also acknowledged that during her college years,
she had been sexual with her boyfriend, gotten pregnant, and hurriedly aborted the pregnancy. She had never worked through those
issues and, in fact, thought it was best to get them out of her mind
and move on with life. "What is past is past," she used to tell me.

In time, her therapy led her to accept the losses in her life and
the great pain and sadness she had held inside about many things.
The cloud of depression started lifting as her spirit was freed from
caged emotions. She began to understand how her depression was
trying to speak to her and draw her toward deep healing.

To do the hard work of exploring the meaning of depression,
you first may need to stabilize your feelings. As Hart and Hart
Weber have recommended, a complete physical exam and psychological exam are helpful to determine the best program for you.
You are worth getting the help you need.

A Time to Accept

Allowing yourself to enter a period of grieving takes patience
and practice. You may fear the process will never end. You may
be struggling to get anything done. The responsible, motivated,
self-directed person you may have always been seems to have dis-
appeared, and you worry she may never return. How will you
function? How will you take care of yourself and your family if
you allow yourself to stay in this place of sorrow?

It is hard enough to grieve without trying to do it alone. Healthy grieving requires validation from others. No doubt some of your grieving and crying will occur in solitude, but when another safe, supportive person witnesses your tears, you can feel the validation of your pain—it is the empathy and compassion of Jesus through another human being. Henry Cloud makes a very important statement about grieving: "Until I found the God who designed grief and got me into the support and structure I needed to face my losses, I did not have losses—I was lost."[4]

Do you feel lost? Do you know how to embrace your sorrow and cycle through the grieving process? I suggest that you first name your feelings and allow yourself to have them: if you are sad, be sad; if you are angry, be angry; if you are anxious or afraid, don't try to hide it. And then give yourself time to live with your emotion. Don't hurry yourself on to something else by getting busy or acting as if everything is all right. Writing or journaling is another helpful way to validate the emotions you are feeling. Ask safe people to listen to you as you share your feelings. And finally, be gentle with yourself. Remind yourself that the grief process is hard work and that you need a great deal of self-care and nurture along the way.

There is a time when you need to take stock of all of the losses that accompany the sexual sin in your marriage. Grieving is not a onetime event. You will move in and out of the elements of grieving and perhaps return to the process even after you thought it was over. But the despair and crying *do* stop eventually. A time will come when you feel finished with grieving. You will experience resolution to your pain, and you will have learned something from the adversity that shattered your life. Moreover, by allowing yourself to grieve, you will have opened yourself up to new energy, new attitudes, and new possibilities.

Finding Purpose in Loss

Not long before my dreams were shattered by sexual betrayal, I read a book by Judith Viorst entitled *Necessary Losses: The Loves, Illusions, Dependencies, and Impossible Expectations That All of Us Have to Give Up in Order to Grow.* I believe today that God was preparing me even then to handle what was coming into my life. Viorst writes, "Throughout our life we grow by giving up. We give up some of our deepest attachments to others. We give up certain cherished parts of ourselves. We must confront, in the dreams we dream, as well as in our intimate relationships, all that we never will have and never will be. Passionate investment leaves us vulnerable to loss.... I would like to propose that central to understanding our lives is understanding how we deal with loss."[5]

I was passionate about my husband, my marriage, and my children. Despite the ways I may have attempted to control the dreams I had for all of us, I couldn't control the pain and loss we would experience. I had much to learn about accepting both love and hate, good and bad, and the inevitable hurt that comes when I get close to someone.

The first significant shattered dream that made a mark on my life was sexual betrayal in my marriage. Living through the losses related to my illusion of a perfect marriage prepared me for other significant losses in my life. I didn't want to think that other tragic losses could be coming my way, but they were. My company faced some terrifying transitions, my children stumbled and fell through their own life choices, loved ones were taken prematurely by illness—and each time I felt more available to the process of loss, of grieving, of acceptance, and of character growth.

Is there a spiritual purpose in facing our shattered dreams? Dr. Larry Crabb, in his book *Shattered Dreams*, helps us look at the purpose in our suffering—in our losses:

> Shattered dreams open the door to better dreams, dreams that we do not properly value until the dreams that we improp-

erly value are destroyed. Shattered dreams destroy false expectations, such as the "victorious" Christian life with no real struggle or failure [or the perfect marriage without work]. They help us discover true hope. We need the help of shattered dreams to put us in touch with what we most long for, to create a felt appetite for better dreams. And living for the better dreams generates a new, unfamiliar feeling that we eventually recognize as joy.

Our pain will always have a purpose. It will not go away, but it will do its work. It will stir an appetite for a higher purpose—the better hope of knowing God well enough now to love him above everything else ... and trusting him no matter what happens.[6]

Many of our lives have been shattered, seemingly beyond repair. Slowly, if we trust God to lead us on, we not only will experience knowing him more intimately; we also will see new growth and purpose emerging from our pain.

Life was still very uncertain for Catelyn. She had been committed to figuring out the problem in her marriage, and after hearing of her husband's sexual acting out, she was committed to seeking God's guidance for her life. She wanted more than anything to stay married to Carl, and yet the confusing days of hopelessness were slowly killing her. Recently, after a meeting of her women's group, she experienced a new kind of joy. She shared this story with me:

I committed myself to the Lord years ago, but last week I felt the deep desire to do it all over again. I gave him my shattered life, the uncertainty of my marriage, and the fear of what would be next for me. I just told him I couldn't control it anymore. Amazingly, I have been overwhelmed with courage to keep working on myself, and I have felt God's love and presence like never before. I have been renewed with my desire to know him and trust him. Also, I continue to witness the insights of who I am. Every day I am led to look at my feelings and triggers. It is as if God keeps bringing them to me for homework! I can't stop sharing with Carl all about *me*—and for the first time, I feel him moving toward me and not withdrawing. I don't get it! I don't know where my life will lead me or how my marriage will be, but I know God in a personal way that I have never experienced before.

Teresa's shattered life has taken her on a spiritual journey, too. She jumped into recovery with all engines firing. She loved the women she was meeting, the new tools she acquired, and the possibilities for change. But she was angry with her husband for his sexual sin, and she stayed focused on that loss for almost a year. When she let go of her desire to recover the marriage of her dreams, God began to work in her heart. Over time she learned to turn inward to her own losses and pain. She had many: abusive parents, critical in-laws, a son who had struggled with alcoholism, and a husband who just didn't "get it" in recovery.

She began to thaw from her bitterness and brokenness and feel the sadness underneath. She processed her shattered dreams and grieved the losses in her life for another year or so. And she clung to God, who became her constant companion and friend. She felt him directing her next steps—small steps.

Today she will tell you that she never knew such joy and contentment could be possible. "I have a whole new life," she says. "I have awareness and compassion and patience and unconditional love unlike I've ever experienced before. And I know God is in all of it. I never thought I could be *grateful* for shattered dreams."

Shattered dreams can lead us to know and depend on God in new ways. They can grow our trust in God that he will make something beautiful out of something that has been terribly painful. Our dream of good relationships with others may very well be replaced with the reality of great relationships with others. We may exchange people-pleasing character for authentic, God-pleasing character. And we may trade our desire for a happy, materialistic life for one of deeper joy and richer relationships—with God, our spouse, our children, our friends and colleagues, and ourselves.

Thinking It Over

1. What fantasies or expectations did you have of your husband and of marriage?

2. What tangible and emotional losses have you incurred because of sexual betrayal in your marriage?

3. What elements of grieving have you been experiencing? Which ones do you try to avoid?

4. Do you think God wants something more for you than what you had before your life was shattered by betrayal—even if your life seemed happy and fulfilled before then? What are some possibilities?

CHAPTER 5

When Will I Stop Feeling So Out of Control?

The Paradox of Powerlessness

Unless I accept my faults, I will most certainly doubt my virtues.
Hugh Prather

My grace is sufficient for you, for my power is made perfect in weakness.
2 Corinthians 12:9

During the first few months after the disclosure of my husband's sexual betrayal, I experienced a period of relative calm. I was finding help, I had friends I could share with, and Mark and I were learning how to talk about our pain together. And then one day during a casual conversation with one of my children, some startling new information came to my attention: "Dad invited one of those women from the health club over to our house when you were out of town last summer. She watched a movie with us—she was just lying on the couch."

Another woman in my house! I couldn't imagine Mark would have done something so outrageous. Another woman on my couch talking to my children! I was enraged.

Flushed, shaking, gasping for air, and determined to let Mark have it, I left the family room to find my husband in the kitchen. My arms were flailing as I shrieked, "I just heard you invited one of the young women from the club to our house when I was gone!" Pointing my finger at him, I demanded that he never again bring another woman into *my* house or around *my* children, or we were done. It was one thing to betray me sexually, but it was another thing altogether to involve the kids.

Compared to the worst of Mark's acting-out behaviors, I'm sure he didn't consider this "movie incident" to be a very big deal. But the drama I was creating in the kitchen made me feel powerful—for a few minutes, at least. I don't even remember if he responded. I didn't really care. I was intent on letting out my rage, and nothing could stop me! I didn't know I had the capacity to be so angry and out of control. I scared myself.

We Are Powerless over Ourselves

Even when our intentions and resolve are aimed in the direction of change, we often find ourselves repeating familiar behaviors and thought patterns no matter how hard we try not to. Being betrayed has probably taken you to some frightening and embarrassing places as well. I've heard women lament, "I don't like what I've become, but I don't think I can change," or "I'm not even sure who I am anymore." Stories of powerlessness can burden our hearts, especially because they illuminate behaviors that most of us would rather not claim.

Several years into my recovery program, I decided to go to bed early one night and read for a while. I fell asleep before Mark came to bed, only to be awakened by what I thought was the smell of smoke. Years ago, Mark smoked a pipe when he was writing his first book. After several "heated" conversations about where pipe smoking would be allowed, *we* decided it wouldn't be allowed in the house, only outside. Since I knew the smell couldn't be from smoking in the house, I immediately panicked, thinking something was on fire. I ran downstairs, only to find Mark and our son coming up from our finished family room in the basement. The smoke I smelled now clearly wasn't from a fire.

When I said I smelled smoke, Mark denied there was any. I felt my whole body fill with anger and hopelessness—I was convinced I had been lied to, and I totally shut down. I didn't say a word. I went back upstairs and pretended to go to sleep. As I lay there, a life-changing awareness hit me: I *could not stop* withdrawing, despite all the work I had done in therapy to be honest with my feelings and voice my needs. Withdrawal was my friend; it was what I had learned to comfort myself with when I was in pain. It was a major way I coped with feelings too difficult to express or manage. I knew intellectually what I needed to do: tell Mark my feelings and my perception of what I saw. But in that moment of feeling unheard again, I was paralyzed. I reverted to a very old, familiar choice.

When I thought about the concept of powerlessness before this incident, I imagined people being out of control with outrageous behaviors: cheating on a spouse, stealing, murdering, lying, taking advantage of people—big things like that. Could subtler, more common behaviors such as withdrawing be evidence of my own powerlessness and inability to respond differently, despite my best efforts to do so? That night I began to see myself with more clarity. In fact, that incident propelled me on a search to uncover the *many* subtle ways I stayed stuck in my woundedness and acted like a victim.

We've discussed the fact that all of our reactions—raging, withdrawing, blaming, hitting, running to a divorce attorney—are ways of coping with our pain. Our husband's sexual sin was a way he was coping with his pain, too. Admitting my powerlessness over my destructive coping mechanisms turned out to be the most important step toward accessing God's power to release me from their grip. I definitely needed a power much greater than me to save me from myself and the behaviors I could not control.

We Are Powerless
over Our Husbands

"I admitted that I was powerless over my husband's behaviors, my emotions, and my reactions, and that my life had become unmanageable." That's my adaptation of the first step of the 12 steps—specifically written for wives working on their own healing from sexual betrayal. If we can take this truth deep into our minds and hearts, then we can find liberation from our painful patterns.

Do you remember the first time you realized you were powerless over your husband? When we feel powerless, we often do what we hate. We are all double-minded, choosing to do those things that hinder intimacy in our relationships, but wishing we wouldn't. Perhaps you can't stop doing detective work and continue searching for evidence of ways your husband has been unfaithful. When you sense he has been *out of control* with his behaviors, you might think you can be *in control* by uncovering what they were. You might insist on taking the lead in getting help for your husband because you need to exert control somehow in the mess of infidelity. And you could demand specifics about his recovery program in an ongoing effort to control him. You might even begin lying yourself or covering up in an effort to control his reputation or consequences. Have you found yourself caught up in any of these efforts, only to realize that you are truly powerless over his behaviors and choices?

It is *hard* to stop controlling others. I tried to control Mark, sometimes wanting to support and protect him, sometimes wanting things to go my way, sometimes afraid he would make choices that would hurt me again. Whatever my motivation, it wasn't healthy. You will hear many people describe a man who has sinned sexually as narcissistic—he is thinking only about himself and not about the pain he is causing others, especially you. There is truth in that portrayal. But as I think more and more about controlling behaviors, I begin to see how narcissistic they are, too. When I'm trying to control someone else, I'm doing it because I need something. I want someone else to change so that I can feel better. It's all about what I need to feel safe, to feel loved, to feel heard.

Susan was scheduled to go out of town on business shortly after she found out about her husband's involvement with Internet pornography. She was anxiously trying to decide what to do. I asked her why it was such a difficult decision to leave. "I need to keep him away from the computer so that he can stay sexually pure," she answered. When I asked her what she would think if she left and he used pornography again, she was quick to respond: "Well, I would have a hard time forgiving myself, because if I want him to stop looking at pornography, then I need to be responsible to help him do that." Susan chose to stay home and sacrificed an important business meeting. Her husband also found ways to continue his pornography use despite her efforts to control him.

Angelica was proud of her husband's choice to participate in a diligent recovery program involving 12-step meetings, therapy, and sessions with their pastor. He spent hours talking with her about his awarenesses, his growth, and his vision for being a new man. She reveled in the attention and devotion he was showing her. But when he began reaching out to other men in his program—which he was encouraged to do by his mentors—she became very angry. She didn't feel as cherished and included in his life, and she began demanding that he stop spending time with these supportive friends. In her therapy group, Angelica was able to admit her controlling behavior and to recognize that by trying to dictate her husband's choices, she was sabotaging his efforts to heal. Furthermore, she was able to talk about her fears and anxiety as she made a commitment to learn to let go of her control.

Sharon tried to control her husband's TV watching. It was excessive, she said. She pleaded with him; she became angry with him; she withheld sex from him. She wanted desperately to have his attention, his companionship—she wanted him to change because she had needs she expected him to meet. It's not wrong to want something from someone else, but we must be careful how we go about getting it. Trying to change others by controlling their behavior never works.

We Are Powerless over Our Triggers

We are powerless over what triggers us and how we initially react to those triggers. A trigger is a stimulus—a look, word, behavior, smell, sound, touch, or event—that reminds us of an earlier experience and creates a reaction. As much as we would like to control our responses to other people and circumstances, doing so is impossible sometimes. We all get triggered, and we simply cannot stop triggers that create reactions.

We can't control triggers by trying to eliminate them from our lives—we'll always be faced with triggers. We can't run away far enough or hide anywhere long enough to keep them away. In the early months of recovery, I loved traveling for my work. By removing myself from our home and Mark, I felt much less triggered by the pain of his sinful choices. Out of sight, out of mind—or so it seemed. The truth was that the triggers were just a little more removed; they weren't gone forever. Being with Mark could certainly bring them back, but so could my own thoughts and memories springing from names, pictures, dates, or places. Dealing with triggers reminds me of trying to keep the weeds from popping up in my garden by putting a thick layer of bark around my perennials. It's only a matter of time before they pop through—they aren't going to be denied their presence! Neither are triggers in your life.

Remember, coping mechanisms are what we use to manage these triggers. If we haven't done much work to understand what triggers us and why, our coping choices will be unconscious and out of control. In fact, we will be so much on autopilot that we won't even know we are coping. We are powerless over our triggers *and* the way we cope with them.

Rosita was watching a movie with her husband, Hermano, several months after he disclosed the affair he had been having for two years. They had been working on healing together and, in fact, were emotionally closer than ever before. During the romantic comedy they were watching, the main character left her spouse for a romantic fling with the neighbor. Rosita began weeping quietly, trying not to let Hermano see her tears. She quickly left the room, saying something about wanting to get some food. She withdrew from him the rest of the evening and couldn't talk about her deep sadness. Since she'd been feeling hopeful about the great progress and healing in their relationship, the trigger in the movie caught her completely by surprise. Her withdrawal was a familiar friend—a coping mechanism she often used when she felt hurt and sad.

Joseph confessed the details of his sexual betrayal to his wife, Florence. She was glad to hear him finally offer the truth about his behaviors. He had lied about many things in their ten-year marriage. In an effort to sort out the many lies, Florence occasionally would ask Joseph a question about his past behaviors. Sometimes he would close his eyes and hesitate while answering. This response infuriated Florence, and she would yell at him and cry out that he must be lying again! She couldn't stop her dramatic reaction—the trigger of possibly being lied to again was very powerful.

We Are Powerless over Our Emotions

We all have emotions, and we have them in all varieties. You may want to control the kinds of feelings you are going to have. Maybe you want only the positive ones to show. You have no problem expressing joy, happiness, contentment, hopefulness, and gratitude. But if a negative emotion comes along, you'd like to figure out how to eradicate it. If you feel sad, maybe you'll just get busy until the feeling passes. The problem is, no amount of busyness will hold back the sadness forever. If your anger is giving you headaches, no amount of medication will take them away. If you are worried about when the next shoe will drop, no amount of hopeful talk will diminish your fears. Your feelings will not be denied. You are powerless over their arrival and sometimes even over their expression.

Wendy was trying desperately to see the good in their lives after learning of her husband's constant struggle with pornography. But each time her husband slipped and admitted to it or was caught accessing pornography, Wendy's sadness grew stronger and less consolable. She tried valiantly to cover it over by serving others and caring for her family. But one day she sat across from me and just sobbed. It had happened once again, and she wasn't able to keep it together this time. The disappointment and hopelessness she'd been feeling had eroded all of her coping skills. She said, "I just don't think I can live like this anymore."

Eventually, if we try to manage our emotions rather than feel them, even the most skilled of us won't be able keep our true feelings submerged. We are powerless over our emotions; they *will* be heard.

The Gift in Powerlessness

Elizabeth Griffin, a marriage and family therapist, and I work together at our counseling center. We have an intern who is finishing her degree in counseling and needs to practice with real clients who have real problems. She also teaches at a local college and understands the importance of setting objectives for where you are going and what you are hoping to accomplish in your class. As we began another group for women betrayed by sexual sin, she asked us, "What is the purpose of your groups?" What a great question! It's good to be reminded of what we are really trying to do—besides support women who are in a lot of pain from someone else's behavior. It's easy to get stuck there and miss the bigger picture. The objective of our work with women is to bring them face-to-face with their own powerlessness so that they can move through the door of brokenness and humility, which is essential for the deepest spiritual transformation.

"Humility?" you might be shouting inside. "What in the world do I need to be humble about? Haven't I suffered enough humiliation already?" The humility I'm talking about is not the same as humiliation. It has nothing to do with embarrassment about someone else's behavior. Humility is about accepting that you are not perfect, that you have flaws, and that you are powerless to fix those things you want fixed, despite your best efforts.

In the Alcoholics Anonymous program, a newcomer is quickly introduced to the concept that the only way to get and stay sober is to begin by admitting complete defeat. AA literature makes clear that this "humble admission of powerlessness over alcohol is [the] first step toward liberation from its paralyzing grip."[1] As recovering alcoholics diligently apply all 12 steps to their disease, they undergo a spiritual transformation of the kind I am convinced is necessary for any of us who are wounded. People who diligently participate in 12-step recovery programs discover that humility brings strength out of weakness and victory out of defeat. "In every case," writes Bill Wilson, cofounder of Alcoholics Anonymous, "pain had been the price of admission into a new life. But this admission price had purchased more than we expected. It brought a measure of humility, which we soon discovered to be a healer of pain. We began to fear pain less, and desire humility more than ever."[2]

If we accept that we are on a spiritual path, that we want God to use us and create purpose in our lives, then we must remember that God calls us to consider our weaknesses—our brokenness and humility. In *The Purpose Driven Life*, Rick Warren speaks concisely on humility and weaknesses:

> Paul gives us several reasons to be content with our inborn weaknesses. First, they cause us to depend on God. Referring to his own weakness, which God refused to take away, Paul said, *"I am quite happy about 'the thorn,' ... for when I am weak, then I am strong—the less I have, the more I depend on him"* [2 Cor. 12:10 TLB].
>
> Our weaknesses also prevent arrogance. They keep us humble. Paul said, *"So I wouldn't get a big head, I was given the gift of a handicap to keep me in constant touch with my limitations"* [2 Cor. 12:7 MSG].
>
> Our weaknesses also encourage fellowship ... [and] show us how much we need each other....
>
> Most of all, our weaknesses increase our capacity for sympathy and ministry. We are far more likely to be compassionate and considerate of the weaknesses of others.... The things you're most embarrassed about, most ashamed of, and most reluctant to share are the very tools God can use most powerfully to heal others.[3]

If we fail to acknowledge and embrace our own powerlessness and need for grace, we will forever stay focused on our spouse and what he did. Some of us may fear that we have to deny our strengths or all of the good we have done in our efforts to lead faithful lives. Some of us may think we have to put ourselves down to accept our weaknesses. But God only calls us to be the human beings we are: unable to manage our lives without him. It is in the honesty of accepting our flaws that we are able to accept God's love and blessing to heal from pain.

The Freedom of Surrender

When we can finally admit powerlessness in our lives, then we can begin to take responsibility for the thoughts, feelings, and behaviors that are hurtful to ourselves and others. As we experience humility by acknowledging these imperfect, incomplete parts of ourselves over which we are powerless, we have the opportunity to experience the freedom of surrender to a losing battle: trying single-handedly to repair the pieces of us that are missing or damaged.

Now that I understand how powerlessness permeates my life, I see examples of it on a daily basis. I am powerless over a multitude of circumstances and behaviors, both mine and others'. I am powerless over my aging body. It is going to wrinkle and sag despite my best efforts to keep it young. My humility can emerge when I realize that my pride keeps me invested in caring more about my appearance than perhaps I want to. I was powerless over the choices Mark made for nineteen years of our relationship together. In my brokenness, I humbly realized that something was keeping me so distracted in my own life that I didn't even see the signs of sadness and loneliness in my own husband. As my children have grown to be young adults, I see how powerless I am over the many decisions they make for their lives. It is humbling to accept that my parenting will never be perfect and that I can't prevent suffering in the lives of those I love the most. I wanted to believe, self-righteously, that if I did my parenting well enough, my children would never have to suffer. Becoming humble has meant accepting my limitations in the areas in which I create unmanageability for myself by trying to exert power where I have none.

When we are aware that we are powerless and broken, we can then practice surrendering—letting go. We've seen that we are unable to control our own lives, let alone someone else's. And it's time to turn over control to the only one who has that power—God. He is the one on whom we need to depend, not ourselves. He is the one who created us and knows all that we are and are not, and he promises to direct our paths and take care of us. But we first must give up our self-reliance.

Surrendering doesn't mean doing nothing—you become a victim when you do nothing. It does mean accepting that you may not understand or like what is happening, but you will choose to take the next step in the healthiest way you know how, trusting God to take it from there. It means taking yourself less seriously and taking God more seriously. The first three of the 12 steps are often summed up this way: "I can't; he can. I think I'll let him."

I had to practice surrender in small ways at first. I practiced with little things such as giving up control of which foods my kids were going to eat and whether they had haircuts as often as I wanted. I surrendered the laundry pile and my efforts to have meals prepared and frozen for the family when I went out of town for work. I gave up trying to make sure my kids' homework was always finished and submitted on time. I surrendered saying yes to things I thought people needed me to do and shopping for "perfect" gifts so that family members would be sure of how much I loved them. I let go of decorating the house to match the holiday season and baking traditional treats that took endless hours I didn't have. I gave up trying to control Mark's time and his ways of doing things.

Then I realized that surrender meant much more. It meant letting go of my husband's decisions and the manner in which he was going to recover from his sexual addiction. I needed to turn those things over to God and his holy wisdom for Mark's healing. I very much wanted to hang on to some sense of control over Mark's recovery, knowing I had a lot to lose if he didn't stay faithful to our vows. But I learned that it wasn't my business to decide if and how Mark would get well. I needed to surrender his pain and his process to God.

I began practicing surrender in the bigger arenas of my life: my career, my kids, my financial security, the health of people I loved, and my future. Surrender meant that I had to let go of my expectations. I had to release my grip on my agenda and my insistence on a particular outcome if I was truly going to trust God to be in charge of my life.

Practicing surrender over and over again leads back around to the first of the 12 steps: to accept powerlessness in my life. I begin to see how many things are out of my control, including other people and their choices—I can't control what other people feel, think, or do. I'd like to think that if I tried hard enough, was smart enough, or persevered long enough, surely I could claim some control. But I'm learning that I simply can't control other people. I don't even have control of my own life. I need to trust God to control my feelings, reactions, and behaviors. All powerlessness, humility, and surrender lead to a deeper trust in God and a stronger dependence on him to guide my life. What a revolution for me! My strengths were doing, organizing, and controlling everything, so practicing surrender was a new way to *trust life.*

Surrender ultimately means accepting that only God, in his great wisdom and perfect timing, will show us the meaning of our situation and the opportunities he is giving us to grow in character. Cultivating our dependence on God leads us to trust more in God. Beginning to live life with God in control proves to be a dynamic and enlivening shift.

The powerful "Serenity Prayer," spoken daily throughout the world by those involved in 12-step groups, is all about surrender: "God, grant me serenity to accept the things I cannot change, courage to change the things I can, and wisdom to know the difference." This prayer was a great reminder to me to start with the little things I couldn't change in my day: "My alarm didn't go off on time and I will be late for work"; "I don't have enough time to call all of the people I care about today"; "I didn't get to exercise like I promised myself I would"; "My husband forgot to tell me about an important engagement." Then the bigger things: "I can't soothe my son's sadness about the direction his career is going";

"A woman I'm working with has made a quick decision to file for divorce"; "I'll never be as comfortable speaking and teaching as Mark is."

Each day is filled with countless opportunities to practice surrender. I invite you to join me in practicing. It will change your character, your relationship with God, and your capacity for intimacy with others. When we find commonality in our powerlessness and brokenness, we can find that connection we long for. When we have been hurt by the behaviors of someone we love, we often get stuck rehashing the same old conversations: "Why did you do that?" "How could you have done that?" "Here's what I'm going to do if you ever do that again." While these conversations provide us with information and boundaries, they won't serve to connect us as a couple. What will connect us is accepting that each of us is on a spiritual journey—each of us is learning how to live out a new kind of humility and learning how to surrender. If we can honor the difficulty of that process, we can begin sharing our hidden heartaches and become allies in our commitment to grow from our pain.

Thinking It Over

1. In what ways do you relate to the concept of being powerless over yourself? Is this experience an unfamiliar one for you?

2. In what ways have you tried to control your husband's behaviors? Did you feel out of control during these times?

3. When have you felt powerless over your triggers and emotions? How have you tried to control your reactions?

4. What negative coping mechanisms do you have that you cannot control?

5. In what small ways can you begin to let go and humbly surrender control of your life or others' lives?

CHAPTER 6

What Do You Mean, "Do I Want to Get Well"?

Looking at Commitment, Risks, and Triggers

Two roads diverged in a wood, and I, I took the one less traveled by.

Robert Frost

Blessed are those who persevere under trial, because when they have stood the test, they will receive the crown of life that God has promised to those who love him.

James 1:12

One of the first questions wives ask me is, "How long do you think it's going to take me to get well?" I think they are usually referring to feeling happy again. In other words, they want to stop crying, stop obsessing about their husband's hurtful acts of sexual betrayal, and stop living with worry. They want to build trust again and feel loved, chosen, and safe in their marriage. Or if their marriage hasn't survived the fallout of betrayal, they want to stop reliving their painful memories, stop feeling paralyzed from the betrayal, and start feeling that they have a life again. The truth is, getting well encompasses much more than any of these goals.

So often we want to find a quick fix so we can get back to some sense of peace. "If only my husband would change his ways and repent, then everything would be all right," we think. But the solution isn't so easy. God uses all of our lifetime experiences to grow us in the likeness of his character. He especially uses trials in our lives to teach us about his love, to challenge our character, and to mature our faith. I ask you the tough question I ultimately had to face myself before any healing could occur in me or in my marriage: Are you willing to surrender to your devastation, the healing process, and whatever outcome God has for you in order to get well?

I first encountered this question at Family Week, but I also remembered that Jesus asked a similar question of someone who once felt as helpless and hopeless as I did. Jesus stood near the pool of Bethesda where the blind, the lame, and the paralyzed lay, waiting for their chance to be healed. Jesus, our great teacher and counselor, didn't ask the questions that I might think to ask: You look very sad and discouraged; can you tell me about that? Have you been hurt by someone? Do you need help to get into the pool? Would you like me to do something for you? Jesus didn't ask any of those questions. He simply asked, "Do you want to get well?" (John 5:6).

What a strange question for Jesus to ask. After all, the man he was addressing had been waiting for *thirty-eight years* to be healed of his paralysis. "I have no one to help me into the pool when the water is stirred," the man answered. "While I am trying to get in, someone else goes down ahead of me" (John 5:7). In much the same way, I lay beside my own "pool" in my anguish, thinking that it really wasn't *my* choice to get well; it was Mark's. "I haven't done anything wrong—why should I have to talk to a therapist or a pastor? What money we have should be used for Mark's healing since his sin is what created this crisis. I wouldn't even need healing if it weren't for his betrayal." And so my thinking went. Despite my reasonable thoughts, however, I remained in misery, blinded, lame, and paralyzed in life and love.

Central to getting well is accepting your part. There is no strained or broken relationship for which one person is totally responsible. I am not minimizing the extreme pain of your husband's sexual betrayal; his sinful choices are unacceptable. I only want to emphasize that somewhere in the breakdown of your relationship, there was a lack of connection and emotional intimacy. Because emotional intimacy always involves two people, part of the accountability belongs to you.

The brokenness, powerlessness, and humility we've talked about in previous chapters are integral to the process of personal and relational healing. Brokenness includes accepting not only what happened to you, but also your own shortcomings and the woundedness that drives you to cope in hurtful ways. Powerlessness means accepting that you carry beliefs about yourself and practice coping strategies that ultimately harm you and others, and that you can't permanently change troublesome things about yourself or others no matter how hard you try. Humility requires embracing these difficult truths wholeheartedly, relinquishing self-reliance, and reaching out to God and others for help and transformation.

When you become willing to get well and do the work necessary to create deeper relationships, one of the most helpful things you can do is own your shortcomings. Doing so is difficult, especially if you have been hurt badly. It's much easier to sit back and keep taking in the apologies of the offender—your husband. Sometimes the pain of sexual sin is so huge that it feels as though you could go on forever riding the wave of entitlement: "I can do whatever I want because I have been hurt so badly." But God doesn't want you to stay in that place. Your growth depends on owning your flaws and failings.

The better you are at being present emotionally in your relationships, the richer your relationships will be. How developed are your tools for emotional intimacy? Do you know the nature of your feelings, and do you express them? Do you ask for what you need? Can you describe your desires? Do you have a personal vision for your life? Can you sort out the mistruths you've been taught and told from the truths you believe about yourself today? Do you know how to initiate or just follow, to be carefree or just

overly responsible, to let go or just control? These and other questions can lead you to examine how you can grow individually to
become the woman God calls you to be. While we are called in our
faith to serve others and to have compassion, we also need balance
in our lives so that we know and take responsibility for ourselves.

When I married, I was young and inexperienced at living life
on my own. I had a lot to learn about myself. I see just as many
wives who married later in life and had already established themselves in successful careers, had many friends, or felt independent in
many ways. But like me, they also realized they had a lot to learn
about themselves and about intimacy. Being independent, asser-
tive, or successful doesn't automatically mean you've accomplished
the tasks necessary for emotional health. In fact, the qualities that
can make you very independent or confident or career driven can
be the same qualities that make it hard to be authentic about your
feelings or to connect emotionally with others.

Deep Cleaning

Shannon participated in our women's group and had an acute
awareness of the level of commitment involved in the process of
getting well. She shared this analogy: "I clean houses for a living.
People can pay me a small amount, and I'll come in and do surface
cleaning. It will look nice for a while and my customer is happy
when I leave. If they want deep cleaning, it's going to cost them
more! But for their money, I'll move all of the furniture and really
clean everything."

Lasting recovery with character transformation requires deep
cleaning. It costs more and takes more time, but it's thorough.
There isn't one right way or one established amount of time that
will lead you to what God wants you to learn. For many of us,
some of the first lessons are about our own impatience. Are we
seeking a quick fix so we can rid ourselves of worry, anxiety, and
unhappiness, or are we to gain something more?

Rick Warren offers some helpful insights in *The Purpose Driven Life* in the chapter entitled "Transformed by Trouble." Even the title suggests that our troubles are templates for learning, not terrible circumstances to avoid.

> God has a purpose behind every problem.
>
> He uses circumstances to develop our character. In fact, he depends more on circumstances to make us like Jesus than he depends on our reading the Bible....
>
> Every problem is a character-building opportunity, and the more difficult it is, the greater the potential for building spiritual muscle and moral fiber.... What happens outwardly in your life is not as important as what happens *inside* you. Your circumstances are temporary, but your character will last forever....
>
> Character building is a slow process. Whenever we try to avoid or escape the difficulties in life, we short-circuit the process, delay our growth, and actually end up with a worse kind of pain....
>
> If you are facing trouble right now, don't ask, "Why me?" Instead ask, "What do you want me to learn?"[1]

If I accepted the fact that I wanted to get well, I would also be accepting the fact that I wasn't perfect and that I had some things to change, too. When I was first faced with all of the hurtful sexual choices Mark had made, I had a hard time seeing that not everything about me was well. I used to say very self-righteously, "For fifteen years I had no idea that Mark was deceiving me and covering up sexual sin." My insinuation was that he had been very, very good at being bad, while wonderful me had led an exemplary life. I eventually and more humbly said, "I can't believe I was so preoccupied with my own life that I didn't even see Mark's pain. I want to know more about what keeps me so disengaged from the people I love."

After I participated in Family Week at the treatment center, I began to see that I did need healing—healing of my own. I decided I didn't want to wait for what Mark or anyone else was going to do. I didn't want to use the leftovers of our resources for my healing. I didn't want to sit back and hope the right people would find me limp and pale and insist on rescuing me. *I wanted to get well.* I determined I would do whatever it took to understand my pain, to let God speak to *me* about what he wanted me to learn and how he planned to grow my character through it. I would trust him and depend on him to take me to places and people who would help me heal. I decided I didn't want to just tolerate betrayal or run from it—I wanted to grow from it.

Everyone's process is unique. I believe that if we choose to accept this journey as a spiritual one, we are asked to be on it until the day we leave this earth. It is a lifelong journey of refining our character to become more like Christ.

Leave Your Comfort Zone

Getting well, or transforming your life, will require you to get out of your comfort zone in many ways. You will need to start doing things that are very new to you, and they won't feel comfortable. You will be tempted to go back to what is familiar and what feels safe. Working on transforming your life means taking risks and changing some things—perhaps many things. All change is a process that bumps you out of your comfort zone. Are you willing to go there?

When I participated in my women's group, I was asked to do all kinds of unfamiliar things—the very first was to start checking in with how I was feeling. Now that may seem easy enough, but honestly, I didn't think or speak that way! I could tell you *what* I was doing, or *why* I was doing something, or *how* I was going to do something, but what I was *feeling*? That was a whole new ball game. I had to readjust my speaking, and surprisingly, when I started naming my feelings, I usually started feeling the feelings—which for me was a very vulnerable thing to do in front of other people. Then I was encouraged to call other women when I needed support, when all I really wanted to do was isolate myself and figure things out on my own. And that was just the start of living out of my comfort zone. Healing was going to take me to places of examination and choices that were very unfamiliar. Could I trust the process?

The bottom line is that getting well is a roller-coaster ride. Just about every wife I talk to describes the ups and downs of her process of healing. That was my experience, too. One minute I felt chosen, listened to, and hopeful—the next moment I was sad, overwhelmed, and discouraged. Sometimes I felt crazy to experience emotions that wouldn't stay put. Some women can't stand the uncertainty of their days and would do just about anything to get back to some sort of calm. Some renounce this journey, saying, "If this is what healing is like, I don't want to get well!"

Feelings that are changing and conflicting are normal, but you can take comfort in the fact that the process won't always be this way. For some couples, a kind of honeymoon period follows the initial disclosure—your husband is doing everything in his power to please you and nurture you in the hope that you won't run away. And after years of living with his distance or absence, you love the attention. You may feel like the chosen princess again! The honeymoon phase won't last, though, if both of you are working to be honest and authentic. Real feelings need to be expressed by each of you. Anger, disappointment, frustration, and resentment surely will be part of the package. You can't reach the connection you desire without sharing these honest but sometimes buried feelings.

I often tell wives that the roller-coaster mode is actually a sign they are moving forward. Most often we arrive at the disclosure of sexual betrayal with many of our emotions covered up—we've learned to make the best of the situation; we can't let others see what a wreck we are inside because they might gossip; we have too much to do to let our real feelings emerge; and so on. So when we finally start letting our real emotions present themselves, they

are all over the map—some up and some down. Although such
emotional expression feels like a roller-coaster ride, really it's the
expression of our authentic self—we are being real about our insides for perhaps the first time.

Jolanda recently came into my office after knowing for two
months about her husband's extensive involvement with pornography and prostitutes. Pieter has been a model client—remorseful,
willing to do whatever it takes to change, connected to Jolanda at
the hip. He doesn't want to be out of her sight, or if he must for
work, he calls regularly to report his whereabouts and his moment-
by-moment agenda for staying sexually pure. Moreover, they have
spent hours talking about the details of his sexual sin, which has
helped Jolanda understand his motives and choices and feel included in his life. She feels a stronger connection to him now than
she has for years, even though it has developed from the pain of
sharing stories of his past. The newfound emotional intimacy has
been thrilling and nurturing. But then without warning she can be
triggered by a reminder of Pieter's betrayal and sink to another low
with feelings of stupidity, distrust, and despair. For weeks, every
time we talked, she started out the same way: "I still feel like I'm
on a roller coaster."

If you decide to get well, you, too, will ride the roller coaster.
Be prepared—it's part of the journey.

Know Your Triggers

I've mentioned triggers many times in previous chapters because
I've found that they are experienced universally—not only by
those of us who have been sexually betrayed, but by every human
being. Usually we think of triggers as hurtful or negative experiences. And usually our reactions are programmed into our auto-
matic response system so that we don't even think about what we
do or why—it just happens.

I became friends with a woman I met on my golf team, and we began to get together frequently because both of our husbands traveled extensively. When she finally met my husband, I discovered my friend had a great desire to write—which is what my husband had been doing for years. She was full of questions and wanted him to help edit her work. I was triggered immediately and felt envy rush through me. I wanted to "keep her to myself" and exclude our husbands from further social gatherings. My brain had pulled up many old memories of pain in those moments. Having grown up with a twin sister, I felt I had lost many friends to Barb once they met her. My perception was that she was more fun, more social, more whatever everyone else admired, and thus I lost out on keeping friends—or so I believed. I found it helpful to look back and understand what triggered my feelings and drove my reaction. When I could link the pain of the past with the trigger of today, I was able to make a different decision when I felt that trigger again.

Triggers always show up when you relate to others. You don't trigger yourself, which is why so many people enjoy being alone—or getting away when relationships get tough. People trigger other people. We remind each other of past pain. Whether the trigger is a look, a word, a behavior, a tone, a touch, or an event, it brings back memories of harm or fear. Your brain is capable of storing memories of every detail of your past, so today when something similar happens, your brain files through your memory bank and pulls up those events or words or looks that belong in the same category, and you get triggered.

Whenever you struggle in your relationships, you can be sure you are being triggered in some way. How we long not to struggle! But if you will allow yourself to struggle and to examine the triggers that your relating is creating, you have the opportunity to grow.

Numerous triggers surface after betrayal. Actually, you experience many triggers every day of your life, but now you are hypersensitive to certain triggers that relate to your current pain. You can be triggered when your husband doesn't listen to you intently, when he is late coming home from work, when he has time for others but not for you, or when he seems interested in touching you only if it leads to sex. You may begin to be triggered by just seeing him! Or by his attempts to say or do anything! Now that you have been hurt, just notice yourself. Triggers seem to pop up everywhere he is—and the desire to escape can be overwhelming at times. Getting away from him seems to be the only way to stop the misery of being triggered.

Nonetheless, triggers are a necessary part of your growth. You must be able to identify them, recognize your reaction to them, assess the way you cope, and think about your needs or desires. You'll also benefit from knowing when these triggers first showed up in your life. While most people want to run away from triggers or figure out a way to eliminate them, I encourage you to move *toward* them. Triggers are like beacons of light that expose our pain. We can't heal pain that we can't identify and discuss. I've actually started using a different word for "trigger" so that it doesn't symbolize something annoying I want to do away with. I prefer to call any trigger in my life an "anointing," meaning a blessing of sorts. When we are "anointed" by a stimulus that opens up a wounded place, we can then begin to understand it, reframe our thoughts about it, and make changes. We experience empowerment and growth when we refuse to let a trigger control our behavior.

When I hear a hurting wife say she needs to get away from her spouse because the betrayal hurts too much, I understand that many triggers are creating intense pain. If someone can help her talk about those triggers and reframe them as anointings, she may be empowered to confront them rather than try to avoid them. But if she just decides to find someone else to share life with, figuring she will meet someone who won't trigger her, it will be only a matter of time before her triggers return. I also know that it can be very helpful to get away from a triggering situation, person, or environment for a time to refresh her spirit.

When you are being vulnerable or building intimacy in your relationships, you are going to get hurt. Getting close means you are eventually going to get triggered, and getting triggered means you will feel pain. Your natural inclination is to pull away from someone who is hurting you or to fight back. But not all words and behaviors that come at you are necessarily meant to hurt you, and you can make conscious choices to develop new reactions.

Detachment is a word often used to describe one way you can choose to take care of yourself when you are feeling hurt or triggered. You remove yourself from the person or the situation; you create distance. Detachment is a way of creating a boundary to protect yourself against hurtful actions or words. You can detach from others in several ways. Some are healthy, and some are not.

You can detach from someone by creating drama or a fight. When you detach this way, you don't have a chance to talk about all of your feelings, fears, or desires, but you do share enough anger that you get the job done—you create distance. Another common way to detach is simply to withdraw. You probably don't say much, if anything; you just decide that sharing space or carrying on any more conversations is too painful. This mode of detachment works temporarily to make you feel safe and to stop the triggers, but you miss opportunities to discuss feelings, needs, and desires.

Compassionate detachment is the term I use for healthy detachment. It allows you to create distance in a relationship for a time but also provides for intentional communication that expresses your honest feelings, needs, and desires. It might sound like this: "I'm afraid of your loud voice and I need to stop this conversation. My wish is that we can figure out a way to talk more constructively." Or you may have a need to refrain from sex with your husband for a time as you work through the emotions of betrayal: "I don't feel like I can be sexual with you right now because I'm hurting so much, but I want to be able to work on a healthy sex life together." Detachment with compassion allows you to practice speaking about your emotions and creating safe boundaries while preserving your relationship.

Certainly you are not to stay attached when in harm's way; in that case, you simply need to get out. But if you are not in harm's way but are simply faced with triggers, you can make different choices. You can set healthy boundaries *and* be compassionate; you can state clearly what you want or affirm any good that you see while also putting healthy distance between you and your husband as you take responsibility to deal with your triggers.

Examine Your Underlying Wounds

Walk with me for a moment, putting aside the sexual betrayal that is now breaking your heart. Let's visit your life apart from all of that tragedy. Perhaps your husband's sexual sin is the event that seems to be responsible for ruining your life. It is the problem that trumps all others. Yet if you answer some of the following questions honestly, you may have a glimmer of recognition that all has not been well.

- What was your life like before you knew about the sexual betrayal? *I WAS PREGNANT*
- Did you have a vision in life for yourself as an individual? As a wife? As a mother? *WIFE / MOTHER*
- Did you feel you were living your vision? *CLOSER TO IT*
- Did you have two or three friends (excluding family members) you could trust with *any* information or feeling? *2*
- Did you feel appreciated at home? At work? *YES*
- Did you feel you were growing and learning? *YES*
- Did you have meaningful relationships at work? At home with family members? With friends? *NOT FRIENDS*
- Did you know what your talents and gifts were? *YES*
- Did you feel your gifts and talents were being used at work? At home? *YES*

- Did you trust people? Men? Women? *YES, USED TO.*
- Were you a proactive person (making plans, making decisions, stating needs, etc.) or a reactive person (responding to others' behaviors and feelings)? Were you satisfied with your role? *YES.*
- Did you take time for yourself? Spend money on yourself? *YES* Take care of yourself physically? Develop friendships? Get enough rest? Get the education you wanted?
- Were you content with where you were in life in terms *NO. WORRIED* of your job? Relationships? Possessions? Opportunities? *ABOUT* Physical health? Spiritual direction? Emotional health? *PREGNANCY*

We could ask ourselves any number of questions about our "wellness" and about any unfulfilled desires we had before the betrayal. I admitted that although my life was wonderful in many ways, it still wasn't without emptiness and discontent. Maybe the ways I coped with the emptiness and discontent distanced me from others I loved and I didn't even know it.

At first I thought that the sexual betrayal had created all of the pain and loneliness in my life. After the initial disclosure, I was bombarded by messages about myself: "I'm not chosen. I'm not enough. I need to take care of myself because no one else will. If Mark would love me, maybe I would be truly lovable." I thought that if the sexual betrayal could be annulled, then all of these messages in my head could be negated, too. But I knew these messages were an ongoing part of my thinking and were causing great sadness for me.

If you truly want to get well from the pain of betrayal, you must be willing to address the pain that is present from other wounds in life, from unfinished pursuits or unmet needs—all of the messages that drive your life.

The truth about willingness is that no one can give it to us, and we can't give it to anyone else. No amount of convincing, threats, sweetness, or pleading can *make* someone decide to get well. You can't make your husband submit to this decision if he isn't willing. Nor can he or anyone else make *you* willing to get well. Perhaps you've experienced the extreme frustration that results when one of you has full-blown willingness to find healing, but the other won't budge. If your husband isn't currently willing to get help, you'll need to exercise supreme patience and allow him the time and space to make that decision. Ultimately you may need to accept that he won't ever be willing.

Mark and I often meet with couples from out of town who are desperate for help with sexual addiction issues in their marriage. They come for three days, and when both are willing, we work through many problems, perceptions, and practical tools for healing. We conducted one recent intensive session with a couple who drove six hundred miles to see us. They made complicated plans to have their three children cared for while they were gone. They spent quite a bit of money to come, stay in a hotel, and be in therapy for fifteen hours. Yet once they were settled in the meeting room, Jason passively leaned over the arm of his chair, distracted with sipping his drink and letting his wife answer all of the questions. He worked halfheartedly on his assignments even as his wife devoted herself to awareness and understanding. Obviously he didn't want to be there. He hadn't made a decision to get well, despite the fact that his wife was ready to divorce him if nothing worked this time.

The scenario is heartbreaking—one person in the relationship is *very* willing, but the other is not.

Signing up for this journey of healing is one of the hardest things any of us can do. Moreover, we are all double-minded in some ways, making our decision that much more difficult. Remember the apostle Paul's conundrum: "I do not understand what I do. For what I want to do I do not do, but what I hate I do" (Rom. 7:15). A part of us likes the place we are in—it's familiar; it medicates our feelings—and a part of us really doesn't like it. But when God wants us to know more, to grow in new ways, to work on some character flaw, he will put pressure on us in one way or another until we surrender to the pain and sign up. It will be his timing, though, not ours.

Expect Battle Scars

Several of my closest friends in life have struggled with a serious cancer diagnosis, including my twin sister. I have learned about getting well by watching them fight for their lives. Getting well has taken on a whole new perspective as I watch them battle physical disease, and I know that battling my emotional "disease" of a broken heart is not so different. They know that really fighting this disease will be a lifelong journey, and some days will feel more peaceful than others. Ultimately, though, they know that it's the big picture that is changing, and they know it's changing everything about the way they live and love and prioritize their lives.

A Journey through Cancer by Emilie Barnes had wisdom for me that correlated my pain with that of my struggling friends and sister. Barnes writes a letter to the reader at the end of one chapter:

> *My Dear Friend,*
>
> *Are you at one of those points in life where you feel flattened, devastated, overwhelmed by grief and loss? It might not feel very comforting right now to be told that you're a prime candidate for the Lord's restoration. But you are.*
>
> *Whether your losses are little or large, they are real and important. It's all right to mourn the years the locusts are eating in your life. . . . Remember, love is a prerequisite for grief. If you didn't love, you wouldn't really suffer from loss. So your suffering in a time of loss is really evidence of your love, and love is always a good thing.*
>
> *In the meantime, if you haven't already begun to see God's purposes at work in your stripping-down time, you might want to consider: Is there something the Lord has for me to learn in this? About humility? About compassion? About appreciation? About letting go?*

I urge you to consciously open yourself to his work. Humble yourself to learn. Open your heart to others. Open your eyes. Open your hands to release whatever it is you're gripping too tightly. Let the locusts have the bitterness and the resentment; you can't afford the negative energy. Focus instead on hope and possibilities.[2]

If you didn't know Barnes's book was about cancer, you would say it was a book about betrayal, wouldn't you? We have common pain and common opportunities if we choose to get well. Barnes also writes, "For me it took something extremely devastating—something that would take me to the deepest depths of self-evaluation—to realize that battle scars are what make someone interesting; battle scars are what make someone wise; battle scars are what make you realize how precious and valuable life really is; battle scars are what prepare you for the inevitable adversity that lies ahead."[3]

I couldn't have imagined it at the time, but my crippling encounter with sexual betrayal is what drew me to the "pool" to find healing from more than just the betrayal. God very effectively captured my attention with the betrayal—and then when I agreed to sign up for the journey, he took me all over the world to shape me into a new woman. I am not without scars, but I am softer, gentler, slower to judge, more spontaneous, more resourceful, more willing to see the story behind the behavior, more open to receive help from others, and more zealous to see how God really wants to use my adversity to make me of maximum service to him.

I desire for you to experience this kind of journey, too. I want your process of healing from sexual betrayal to be an opportunity for you to become the woman Christ calls you to be—the woman who has the capacity and commitment to love outrageously and live contagiously.

Thinking It Over

1. Do you want to get well from the sexual betrayal in your marriage? If not, what is preventing you from making that choice?

2. Do you feel as though you are on a roller coaster? What do you do when you are up? When you are down?

3. In addition to sexual betrayal, have other things in your life been unwell? Parenting? Work? Finances? Sex? Spiritual life?

4. What triggers you the most? Can you identify certain feelings you have when you are triggered? What do you do when you are triggered?

5. In what ways is your character already being refined by the sexual betrayal in your relationship?

CHAPTER 7

How Can I Ever Trust Him Again?

The Million-Dollar Question

As soon as you trust yourself, you will know how to live.

Johann Wolfgang von Goethe

Trust in the LORD with all your heart and lean not on your own understanding; in all your ways submit to him, and he will make your paths straight.

Proverbs 3:5–6

Here is the million-dollar question you are no doubt asking: Will I ever be able to trust my husband again? I never talk to a woman who has been sexually betrayed who isn't thinking about restoring trust. It seems that all hope for restoring a marriage betrayed by sexual sin rests on your ability to trust your husband again. "If I can't trust him," you may be thinking, "then I can't love him, stop my controlling, or commit to anything in the future." These are paralyzing thoughts because they require someone else to be or do something before you can feel all right and make choices you feel good about.

Like everything else we've considered so far, rebuilding trust is a process. I talk to women who think they need to trust again as soon as possible—literally weeks or months after the disclosure of sexual betrayal in their marriage. Ella came to see me just one month after she found her husband's large stash of pornographic magazines. He hadn't admitted that his use of pornography was a problem, nor had he apologized for any harm it had done to their relationship. He was actually angry that she was so bothered by the discovery, but he did agree to talk to a therapist. When Ella talked with me, she cried through her story, then blurted out, "I can't seem to trust him now. I know I should." I asked her why she thought she should trust her husband so quickly. She didn't know. She dropped her head and mumbled that she was a Christian and he was her husband, so she assumed she should trust him.

Donna came to group announcing that her husband had been a "saint" since he broke her heart with information about a two-year-long affair he had ended. He did everything possible to get help and make positive changes in his life. She even told all of us that he was so patient with her rage and her obsessive nature that she couldn't believe he could put up with her day after day. Donna was a devout Christian, so she surprised us by revealing that she didn't think she could ever forgive him even though he was living differently now. Her biggest battle was figuring out how she could trust him. She was never able to make progress in our group. I sensed that she remained stuck in her process because deep down she harbored feelings of anger and resentment she had no intention of giving up. As long as she was angry, she could create distance. And until she was willing to accept the loss and sadness that lay beneath her anger and work on healing those emotions, she wouldn't want to be close to her husband no matter how hard he tried to regain her trust. She was sabotaging any progress in rebuilding their relationship.

What does trusting your husband after sexual betrayal really mean, anyway? Does trusting him mean that your husband will stop all sexual behaviors? Or thoughts? Or glances at other women? Does it mean he will never lie or distort the truth or hide anything from you again? Does it mean he needs to live a perfect life before you can begin loving him again?

When I married Mark, I handed him a big chunk of myself labeled "My Trust." I just gave it over to him. We didn't discuss why I did that or what it meant; I just thought exchanging marriage vows meant never having to think about trusting my husband again. I blindly trusted everything he did and said; I never questioned anything. If at times I wasn't happy or satisfied, I assumed something was wrong with me. I had a very naive, undeveloped concept of trust. Trust just existed: you didn't have to work at it; you didn't have to earn it; it was there until someone broke it.

Now, many years of growth down the road, I understand better what marital trust means to me. In trusting Mark, my motivation is to grow emotionally, spiritually, and physically close to him. I want to know him like no other person gets to know him; and I want him to know me like no other person knows me. Trusting is about wanting to be vulnerable with him without getting hurt. If I can't trust what he is saying, where he is going, whom he is with, or what he is doing, I will stop sharing myself with him. My desire to know him and be known will shrivel up until I lose all hope that we are truly special to each other. I seek to be a trustworthy person and to live with a trustworthy person so that both of us can grow and experience the deepest intimacy possible as husband and wife.

I'm sure trust was broken in many small ways throughout my marriage; I just didn't look at it that way: when Mark's time couldn't be accounted for, when stories didn't exactly match up with the facts I knew, when promises were broken because work seemed to trump everything else. Trust was broken in a lot of little ways. Although I may have had feelings about those minor trust breaks, I didn't express them. I didn't listen to my intuition that something was wrong.

These minor trust breaks always involved some type of cover-up—either outright lies or lies of omission. But because they were so small, I usually minimized them or denied their importance. Trusting to me meant blindly believing that Mark would be honest about everything—what he was thinking, where he was going, whom he was with, what he was doing. I thought that by trusting him I would automatically be clued in to everything about my husband. It was almost as if I wanted to own him in some ways—as if he belonged to me because I was married to him.

Then the bomb dropped that shattered my naive trust of almost two decades. I was shocked to learn of my husband's behaviors, because they just didn't fit the man I thought I knew and loved all those years. But I was almost more shocked to realize that he had lied to me our entire married life. I've heard countless women say that being lied to is harder than being betrayed sexually. I would have to agree.

The problem with lying is that you begin to question the truth about everything. If Mark had lied about his sexual sin, what else had he lied about? Whether he loved me? Whether he was happy? Whether he was doing what he really wanted to do? Whether he planned to stay married? Whether he really enjoyed his family? When a spouse's lying has been exposed, even everyday kinds of moments get scrutinized.

Rachel said that her family had enjoyed a fun outing to the park that weekend, but while they were there, she wondered whether her husband was truly having a good time or just faking it. Rebuilding trust after betrayal has as much to do with desiring honesty in all aspects of your relationship as it does with desiring sexual purity.

The Value of Full Disclosure

How does your husband build trustworthiness after it has been decimated by sexual betrayal? The first thing I wanted after the initial disclosure was to hear Mark confess his wrongdoing. I needed him to own the specific sexual acts that broke our marriage vows.

Even after shattered dreams are discussed openly, women can still feel confused, distraught, and angry. Something doesn't feel right. When I ask them if they know all of the details of their husband's acting out, they often say they aren't sure. They may have found out about some of his behaviors, but they still feel uncertainty in their minds and uneasiness in their bodies.

Incomplete disclosure of sexual betrayal can make wives feel crazy. When a husband is still keeping secrets, a certain "energy" in the relationship reverberates with deception. More often than not, this tension triggers paranoia in a wife. She may become a private investigator because she needs to make sense of the discord she experiences between what she knows (or is afraid she doesn't know) and how she feels as she tries to trust the man who betrayed her. Off she goes in search of the facts—secrets she believes her husband is still hiding. But detectives don't make good companions, and suspicion prevents connectedness. Constantly being on high alert for any hint of possible deception doesn't promote healing in a broken relationship.

If you are experiencing any of these feelings or behaviors and want to experience real healing with your spouse, I recommend *full disclosure* on your husband's part. Knowing the whole truth is foundational to building a new life together because the new structure must be built on honesty and openness. And it doesn't require *you* to uncover all the facts.

When Mark and I work with a couple preparing for full disclosure, Mark helps the husband create a timeline of his entire life and his sexual development and activity, including sexual awakening, sexual abuse, sexual experimentation, and sexual relationships. Eventually he shares these details with his wife. I work with the wife to establish boundaries regarding the information she wants and needs to know. She needs to have the right motivation for the questions she asks. We also talk about her expectations of the disclosure session. During full disclosure, the husband has an opportunity to talk through his timeline uninterrupted. After that time, his wife may respond with any feelings she has or questions she wants to ask. Often new information comes out, even when a wife thought she knew it all. And sometimes that new information can devastate the wife all over again.

The purpose of full disclosure isn't to create more trauma and anger and hopelessness. Rather, the purpose is to reveal the whole truth. No one can rebuild trust on a foundation cracked with lies. While most of us want to heal from betrayal and find a way to forgive, none of us is willing to continue living with deception. We need the truth about the past. We need a commitment to truth telling in the future. And we need a place to start. Full disclosure can give us that starting point—even though it can be extremely painful.

Christine and her husband had been working very hard in recovery after Nathan disclosed an instance of sexual acting out two years earlier. Nathan finally admitted to additional information he hadn't shared with her. Trusting now that Christine was going to stay in the relationship, he was ready to complete his disclosure at their next couple's therapy session. He revealed that he had visited prostitutes and stolen money to pay for them—activities that were far more hurtful to Christine than the pornography and masturbation she already knew about. Although Christine was notified before the session that its purpose was for Nathan's further disclosure, she had no idea that the new information would be so traumatic.

The next six months were rough for this couple. Christine had more losses to face, and her anger resurfaced. The whole process launched her into more grieving, which by now she accepted as a necessary part of her healing. Very slowly she emerged from her sadness and anger and began to work at trusting again. In the meantime, Nathan surrounded himself with the support of other safe men, and with their help, he was able to be patient and allow Christine her space to heal.

Even though full disclosure poses a severe test to your relationship, at least you know you have heard everything there is to hear and there should be no more surprises. You know what it is you need to grieve, and you are free to make the decisions you need to make for yourself. Have the health risks been too great? Have your best friends been involved? Have inordinate amounts of money been squandered? Sometimes the sexual betrayal has been so damaging that nothing can convince you to stay. Full disclosure gives you the freedom to make that choice. At the same time, your husband can stop living with secrets that keep him hiding his behaviors, lying, and walking on eggshells in fear of your finding out. It is an honest place for both of you and the only place that allows solid rebuilding and permanent transformation.

When Mark and I were working on healing together, no one encouraged full disclosure. Although most of Mark's disclosure was accomplished at the treatment center, additional pieces of information came to light in later conversations and sent me reeling with anger. Each time something more came out, I sank to a new low. I remember a counseling session with Mark's colleagues that was intended to reconnect us in a healthier relationship. We were planning to share our feelings, talk about forgiveness, and strengthen our emotional intimacy. But shortly into the session, someone mentioned a woman who had been helping Mark with research. Mark had previously identified her as someone with whom he had had inappropriate sexual contact, but now I was hearing from someone else about a time they'd been together in another city—information that was new to me. I lost it! I can't even describe how out of control my emotions were. To this day, I don't know what else happened during that session. I just knew that receiving information by means of the "installment program" was killing me.

If you've been a party to the installment program, you know the pain I'm talking about. You also know its detrimental effects on rebuilding trust: when information keeps leaking out, your *desire* to trust is undermined. Sometimes the installment program is intentional. Your husband gives you a little information to test your reaction and to see if you will stay. Then he reveals a little more. Breaking the news to you slowly might seem like the easiest and safest way to move toward full disclosure. This method is probably the most common one men use to uncover their secrets. Rarely do I see a husband bare his soul with total honesty and disclosure. I remind wives that if he had the ability to be completely honest and vulnerable, then he probably wouldn't have been acting out sexually in the first place.

Other times the installment program is unintentional. For husbands whose acting out has spanned many years, remembering every detail can be difficult. In our case, certain incidents that happened over nineteen years would be important to me but were overlooked during Mark's initial disclosure. I remember being on a business trip ten years into our recovery. I was listening to some tapes from various conferences, and Mark was telling his story on one of them. He mentioned a specific detail of a sexual encounter that was new information to me—ten years later! For about fifteen minutes, my heart raced and I felt traumatized all over again. Fortunately, I thought to call Mark right then and talk about my feelings and reaction. He was able to hear me, answer my questions, and acknowledge my disappointment. Knowing he hadn't intended to omit this information, I was able to let it go and not allow it to destroy the rest of my trip or undermine the intimacy we had built.

If your husband has already decided to file for divorce, is in another relationship, or simply refuses to get help, you will have to accept huge gaps of missing information that would validate your reality. You may never know the whole truth about his sexual betrayal. Such incomplete knowledge can make you crazy, because your body, mind, and soul want congruency; all parts of your being want to be aligned in reality.

When Carmalita joined our group recently, she was inconsolable in her anger and pain. Her husband had left her and their three children, including a six-month-old baby, for another woman. He

was planning to divorce Carmalita and had already begun proceedings. He'd quickly moved out and was already living with his
affair partner. He refused to talk about anything or seek counseling, saying only that he didn't love her anymore. When she came
to therapy, she was like a caged tiger who hadn't eaten in a month.
Whenever he came over to discuss some divorce issue, she pinned
him to the wall demanding that he tell the kids why he was leaving
them. She hit him, spit at him, and clawed his arms in the hope
that he would share something. She needed desperately to be heard
and validated.

In the context of safe community, Carmalita gradually learned
how to talk about her reality—the unfairness, the frustration, and
the selfishness of her husband's decisions—and we helped her accept that she probably never would fully understand his motives,
his thoughts, or the needs that drove him to choose to leave her.
Letting go of trying to be heard by her husband was a big step
toward sanity and serenity for Carmalita. Finding other people
who could help her piece together her reality and her response to
the situation was critical to her healing. Although surrendering to
the truth that she would never know all of the facts was extremely
difficult, it led her to a spiritual transformation that enabled her to
find peace in the midst of her unknowing.

The Power of Active Repentance

Once Mark had disclosed to me the full scope of his sexual sin,
I needed to know that his sinful sexual behaviors had stopped. I
needed to see that he was remorseful. I needed to witness his sadness and shame to validate his repentance. When I saw that he was
broken, I could begin to trust his desire to get help. By watching
his repentance in action—his willingness to do whatever it took to
change and get well—I became willing and able to trust *the intent
of his heart*. This was a turning point for us.

When remorse is real, change comes from the heart. A man with a heart change acknowledges the hurt he has caused and owns his sinful behavior. He is more patient, more gracious, and more eager to seek God's wisdom and direction. In short, he is different. I was fortunate to witness Mark's heart change immediately after disclosure. He was visually broken and verbally remorseful. He faced many consequences and stopped running from the truth. I had no doubt that his spirit was broken, that he desired help to change his life, and that his intent was not to hurt me anymore.

In this early stage of healing from sexual betrayal, it's crucial that you trust the intent of your husband's heart if he expresses genuine remorse. As much as you would like for him to live a perfect life now—be sexually pure, never lie again, never distort the truth, always share his feelings, never keep a secret, and so on—that wish simply isn't realistic. He is human; he is not God. All of us make mistakes, even if we are committed to being upright and trustworthy in every situation. Your husband will never be perfect, and if you're honest, you'll admit that you're not perfect either. But if you can trust the intent of his heart, you can learn to process the imperfections by talking about them honestly. If you notice his schedule doesn't match what he told you, you address the incongruency. If he appears to be gazing at another woman, you share your feelings. Processing means that *you* are honest about *your* feelings, needs, and desires—and ideally your husband will stay connected to you by doing the same.

The next step for me in reestablishing my trust in Mark was to see him participating in a program to help him stay sexually pure. I needed him to take the lead in becoming a trustworthy person. Since he was the one who had broken trust, I needed him to work at restoring trust. He was in charge of determining ways he could redeem his credibility with me. It wasn't my job to figure out what he needed to do to prove his desire to be sexually pure. If he was truly remorseful and broken, he needed to show it by being willing to go to any lengths to rebuild trust in our relationship.

Here are some of the lengths Mark went to for me: He was willing to let me know where he was at all times without my asking, which demonstrated that he wanted to be considerate of me. He was also willing to let me know whom he was with, and if he had to spend any time with a woman, he let me know he was creating safe boundaries by including other men. He was willing to let me know his email password and check his cell phone activity if I desired. (Please remember that I don't advocate doing detective work—a husband's *willingness* to share any and all information is what is important here.) He was willing to include me in all financial information: the location of all of our money, credit card bills, phone bills, cash withdrawals from bank accounts, and so on. To reestablish his trustworthiness, he readily included me in all of the ways that I had been excluded in the past.

If your husband is willing to do whatever it takes to rebuild trust, then he will be open to listening to your hurt and pain, even when he is tempted to run away or defend himself. I needed to practice how to share my feelings when I was triggered: "I just answered a phone call for you from a woman who didn't identify herself. When you finished talking to her, you didn't offer me any information about who she was or why she called. I'm angry she wasn't more considerate, and I'm sad you wouldn't think to include me in that information. It feels like a cover-up and reminds me of old patterns we had."

Usually Mark patiently heard my feelings and acknowledged them without defending or explaining his behaviors: "I can see you're angry and sad, and I understand why you would question who was on the phone. I'll try to tell you who I'm talking to if it happens again. I'm sorry—I don't want to hurt you." This process is a two-step in trust building—you clearly state your triggers and feelings, and your husband hears you and validates your feelings.

If your husband is doing whatever it takes to be a trustworthy person, he will need to have accountability—other safe men who are invested in accompanying him in his quest to be sexually pure. If he is broken and remorseful, he will know he can't make the changes he desires by himself. Your husband may wish for you to be his only accountability person. He might feel safer not involving anyone else in his secret life because doing so would be too embarrassing for him or threatening to his career. But if you are his only accountability partner, your husband won't change in the ways he needs to. The relationship you are seeking is that of husband and wife, not mother and child. Someone to whom we are accountable may tell us things we don't want to hear, or give us advice. As a wife, you don't want to be the one creating your husband's boundaries, talking through his temptations, and checking up on him. Playing this role can't possibly produce the intimacy you want. Real and lasting trust can be built only when your husband is committed to finding safe men for accountability and companionship as he works to be sexually pure.

Practical Tools for Restoring Trust

When beginning to recover from sexual betrayal, a wife needs to know daily that her husband has stopped his sexual acting out. Some are afraid to ask because their husband gets angry and defensive when they do. Others want to avoid "being his mother" by constantly asking him questions. To avoid these pitfalls, Mark and I suggest a checking-in process called FANOS, an acronym derived from a Greek word meaning "to shed light on" or "to bring to light." It not only brings to light the nature of sexual purity, but also provides a way for a couple to connect emotionally—bringing light to each other's hearts.

Each letter of the acronym represents a subject you will talk about together:

Feelings: Share with your spouse a feeling you have.

Affirmations: Affirm your spouse for something he or she has done.

Needs: State a need you have today (not necessarily one that must be met your spouse).

Ownership: Take responsibility and apologize for something you have said or done.

Sobriety: Here your husband has an opportunity to tell you the status of his sexual purity that day. You have an opportunity to check in regarding something you are working on (sobriety from overeating, raging, criticizing, withdrawing, etc.).

One of you will begin the check-in and run through your entire FANOS; then the other will do the same. Talking through the entire FANOS should take no longer than a few minutes, but it gives you both a regular opportunity to share what you are thinking, feeling, and doing on your journey toward healing from sexual betrayal.

Vicky carried out the following FANOS with her husband; it provides an excellent example to follow.

Feelings: I'm a little scared but hopeful. I've gotten used to being alone for the past two months. I'm worried about the conflict when we move back in together.

Affirmations: I'm thankful for your demeanor during counseling today. You seemed quiet, settled, and kind. I felt loved and heard.

Needs: I need some recognition from my boss that I helped solve a big problem for the company last week. I took a big risk to be honest and report some inappropriate conduct, and I realize I want to be thanked.

Ownership: I'm sorry that I have yet to recognize many issues from my family of origin. In particular, I regret my financial phobia. You're a generous man. We could have resolved our financial issues if only I hadn't been so

sensitive. I believe my conduct has harmed us, and I'm
sorry about it.

Sobriety: I've practiced healthy eating habits all day. While I
have occasional periods of hunger, I'm making progress in
being more honest about how I've used food to cope with
my feelings.

Another concrete way for a couple to rebuild broken trust is to
talk frankly about the dynamics that typically led up to a husband's
sexual infidelity, especially if his infidelity had become a pattern.
As Mark began to understand the patterns of his sexual sin, he re-
inforced his renewed commitment to our marriage vows by sharing with me boundaries he was creating to protect himself from
acting out again. He needed to change certain rituals, including
behaviors that weren't directly associated with sexual choices. For
instance, when Mark was overloaded with work responsibilities,
he felt entitled to treat himself with some kind of pleasure. If I was
unavailable because of my work or the kids, he would turn to other
sexual pleasures. Numerous triggers were part of the cycle that led
Mark down the slippery slope of sexual sin, and our relationship
improved once he identified these triggers and established a plan
to protect himself with appropriate boundaries.

Karen's husband shared frankly with her in a similar way. Ted
typically fell into affairs with women while traveling for business.
As he dissected his cycle of sinful choices, he told Karen it started
during happy hour when he would have a few drinks and then
become flirtatious with other women. He was already tired from
the day and bored with evening hours to fill in his hotel room.
The combination of alcohol, tiredness, and boredom led him into
a cycle he couldn't stop. Choosing to give up social drinking when
traveling and to replace cocktail hour with working out was a way
he began rebuilding trust with her.

If you are ready to begin trusting again and your husband has
joined you by doing whatever it takes, you should think about the

things you need that he may not have thought about. While ideally he will be working hard to earn back your trust, you may find that your fears or anxieties are calmed when you make specific requests. For example, when Mark and I were in public together, I asked him to introduce me to women who might come up and talk to him. (He had quite a few community responsibilities, so it wasn't uncommon for people to approach him.) Susan asked her husband if he would call her each night before he went to bed when he was traveling. Nancy needed to know that she could ask questions about women at her husband's workplace if she felt triggered when she saw them. You don't always get your needs met in the moment, but it's healthy to keep identifying your needs and asking for a response. If you learn to ask in a nondemanding, noncritical way, your husband should be willing to try to meet your needs in the interest of rebuilding the trust he has broken.

Trust versus Control

Trusting your husband means relinquishing his life to him and allowing him to be responsible for his life and actions. It means believing that you will be all right no matter how he chooses to be responsible for himself. It doesn't mean you will always like his decisions, agree with them, or be willing to live with them—but you will be able to make decisions for yourself and know intuitively what next steps you will need to take.

You may feel the only way you can trust your husband again is to know about everything he is doing and to regulate his time, his computer use, his behaviors, and his choices—to have power over every aspect of his life. You may think you can maintain power over your husband as a consequence of his betrayal, but this kind of control never develops the kind of trust you seek in your marriage.

You may be tempted to control your husband if and when he shares his plans and promises with you. When you have been entrusted with information, you may decide you now need to monitor it. So you watch for inconsistencies, point out mistakes, criticize less-than-perfect attempts to do things differently, and judge whether his efforts are enough. Before you know it, you're back into an old pattern that drives you and your husband apart: out of your fears and anxieties, you attempt to control, leaving your husband feeling as though he can never do anything right.

So what can you do when your husband's behaviors are not okay and you can't seem to trust him? Andrea's husband hadn't been to any therapy or support group for a month. He wasn't sharing anything except his work schedule, and she had no idea whether he was still looking at pornography. She didn't want to control his program, but she wasn't satisfied with the way things were.

Andrea can choose to share her feelings, needs, and desires: "I'm lonely, frustrated, and concerned. I need to know you're being sexually faithful to me and that you're serious about doing whatever it takes to stay pure. I want to work at improving our relationship and stay married." And then she needs to let go and allow her husband to do his own work. She can decide what she can and cannot live with and how she will cope in healthy ways.

The problem with building your trust based on what you *see* your husband doing—or not doing—is that you will always see room for improvement. In the first year or two of recovery, I was most interested in seeing that Mark was sober, that he was committed sexually to me only. When it was evident that he was, I started seeing other things that bothered me. Could I trust that he was telling me the truth about his travel schedule? Was he truly forgetting details that created havoc with my work schedule? When Mark shared information about our life that I would have preferred keeping to ourselves, I wondered if I could trust his boundaries about talking to others. As you work to reestablish trust after sexual betrayal, you open doors to many other topics that call for openness and dialogue.

Tuyen's husband hadn't used pornography for years, and yet she found herself wondering if she could trust him to parent effectively.

Ellen was assured that her husband was committed to a sexually pure life, but she had many doubts about the way he handled the family money. When trust issues beyond sexual betrayal surface, remember to keep the goal of your process in mind. You can't go from distrusting your husband to trusting him unconditionally, but you can learn to talk about what you see and hear and to have healthy conversations about what triggers distrust.

Of course there will be deal breakers—behaviors that drive you to determine that you can no longer stay in your marriage. You don't have the power to change your husband; only he can make decisions to change. Your trust in him will grow if he chooses to work on his issues, but just as important, your trust in yourself will grow as you work on yourself and practice owning your behaviors, letting go of other people's choices, and sharing your feelings, needs, and desires—in other words, being responsible and authentic. Every time you practice, you demonstrate your ability to take care of yourself.

Trusting Yourself

Jane was distraught that her husband couldn't stop looking at pornographic videos when he was taking care of their young child. She was weeping when she said that she just wanted to trust her husband. "I can't live without him; I need him to be sober to be able to help raise our son." Jane had huge fears about being a single mom. She and her husband had separated for several weeks before, and she was almost incapable of getting to work and taking care of her son. I'm sure she wanted her husband to be trustworthy for her, but a burdensome fear also motivated her to make him trustworthy because she didn't believe she could manage life on her own.

Maria's situation was similar. She was a stay-at-home mom who hadn't worked outside the home for more than ten years. She was satisfied to let her husband manage all of their assets since he was a successful lawyer. She confided to her group that she desperately needed to be able to trust her husband because there was no way she could support herself.

Kirsten had been married ten years to her first husband. They had two children, and during their marriage, Kirsten had risen in her company to become very financially independent. Her husband was a practicing alcoholic and also used pornography regularly. Kirsten eventually tired of the distance that grew between them and resented his lack of attention to her, so they divorced. Within three years she met and married Kyle. He showered her with his time and devotion, and she was convinced she had finally met the man of her dreams. Only two years later she found receipts that revealed the secret promiscuous life he had been living the entire time they had been married. Kirsten was fully capable of living alone and providing financially for herself and her children. But she began to doubt that she was lovable enough or sexual enough to be cherished by any man. Kyle was the second husband, along with two previous significant others, who had betrayed her. She didn't trust her own worthiness.

Trusting yourself includes being honest about your feelings and triggers, even if you find it easier to withdraw and hide your genuine feelings or to rage and let your emotions run wild. Getting triggered means you are in some painful place, and working through your anguish means you will have to talk about it. You may need to have women to support you when you need to vent, or you may need to clear your mind before engaging in conversation with your husband. Trying to figure out all of your triggers alone isn't healthy. Sorting them out in safe community is part of the accountability *you* need. As you can see, building trust is not a passive enterprise!

If you have needs you are convinced only your husband can meet, you will desperately need him to live a perfectly trustworthy life — no slipups, no mistakes. When he fails to be perfect, the very foundation of your life is shaken. You not only don't feel chosen and included by him, but you may not feel safe either. You may begin to worry about how you will take care of yourself if your husband doesn't get his act together. Out of your immense need to feel safe or cared for, you will most likely be demanding, critical, and controlling of his behaviors in an attempt to *make* him perfectly trustworthy. Unfortunately, we can't make someone be trustworthy—and no one can be perfect. The goal in trusting yourself is to know that you can and will be okay even if your husband isn't everything you want him to be.

Katie was still reeling from the losses she felt after her husband's disclosure. They had had a very active sex life together. It was very fulfilling, she said, for both of them. Now Bill had admitted he had been with many prostitutes and had used pornography for years. "He has ruined my sexuality," she cried out to the women in her group. "I don't know how I will ever reclaim my sexuality again." Her sense of loss was real. She felt robbed of her sexuality because it was no longer unique to how she experienced it with her husband. She felt as though someone had literally taken away something she *owned*. Only as she learned to trust herself did she discover that this perception wasn't true.

Trusting yourself means knowing the truth about who you are based on how *you* define yourself, not on how someone else does. No one else can give Katie her sexuality or take it away. She does own it. As a person, you can be blamed, belittled, or betrayed—but that doesn't mean those words or behaviors *are* you. When you work at trusting yourself, you won't allow other people to take things from you—literally or figuratively—or determine who you are. Only you hold the power to do that.

Trusting yourself means assessing your fears and anxieties, then working to grow in ways that eliminate or manage them. It also means believing that only you have the authority to define you. What your husband has done or said doesn't *take away* who you are. Moreover, what he does in the future doesn't define you either!

As you learn to trust yourself, you will have confidence that you will be okay even if your husband (or anyone else, for that matter) lets you down or proves to be untrustworthy. But trusting yourself doesn't mean you won't feel hurt, angry, or sad again. While you might have to make new decisions, you can trust your ability to create safe community and learn skills to manage your life. If you've been working hard to be vulnerable with other people, you will know how to identify your needs and ask for help. You will also be able to create safe boundaries for yourself, even if others around you don't have safe boundaries. When you can trust yourself this way, you can allow your husband to be human (and other people too); you don't need him or others to be perfect for your life to be all right.

Taking Care of Unfinished Business

Often a woman who is in relationship with an unfaithful man has experienced similar unfaithfulness from some other man in her life. If certain roadblocks seem to sabotage your ability to trust when you really want to, you may find it helpful to examine your past for unfinished business.

Rebuilding trust doesn't just happen; you and your husband both need to work at it. Your part involves demonstrating to yourself that *you* are trustworthy, as well as making a decision to trust your husband again. Until you are ready to make that decision, you may unconsciously sabotage your husband's efforts to restore trust.

Looking back at your history to gauge the trustworthiness of other men in your life can be very helpful. If you have been abused or abandoned by any men or boys in your life, your trust in men has already been tested. You may have thought your husband was finally going to be the man you could trust completely—and now even he has broken your heart.

If you have a significant history of unfaithful or abusive men in your life, you will need to do some work to heal old memories and messages. If you carry the message that men simply aren't trustworthy, your husband will have difficulty earning your trust even if he works diligently at being a trustworthy person. You may cling to your anger and hurt like a protective garment, despite his efforts to make amends and hear your feelings. Some of those feelings could very well be connected to the men in your past. If so, your husband alone cannot heal your wounds.

Amanda's father was unfaithful to her mother throughout their life together. He had been married to another woman before he met and married Amanda's mother, but he chose not to tell her of his previous wife and two sons. After he died, Amanda's half brothers (whom she met for the first time as an adult) lied about their father's wishes and were successful in excluding Amanda from the inheritance money that was left to the children. In addition to the breaches of trust Amanda experienced in her family of origin, her four significant boyfriends all cheated on her sexually. When she recently found out that her husband had been secretly visiting Internet pornography sites, she felt outraged and hopeless. She couldn't imagine ever trusting him again. In fact, she admitted in counseling that she actually hated men. To develop trust with her husband, Amanda will need to heal from the pain of her past.

Look at the patterns of trust that show up in your life. You can work at changing your capacity to trust when you have more information about your historical experience with trust. Also look at your other current relationships to see how trust has been broken and how you reacted and restored trust with those people.

Dealing with Slips and Relapses

For over two years, Nick had been participating in a rigorous program of sexual purity, attending 12-step meetings, and going to therapy. After moving and taking a new job, he slid back into old patterns of looking at pornography at work and was caught. The consequences of his relapse were serious—he lost his job for a second time.

Michael had been faithful to Mallory for several years after confessing to numerous affairs. When tragedy struck and his son and his father died unexpectedly from cancer, he fell into another affair with a colleague at work. He, too, relapsed into significant old patterns of sexual acting out.

What distinguishes a slip from a relapse is frequency and intensity. A slip is a short lapse in progress. For a man who has been struggling with pornography, a slip would involve visiting an Internet site after months of abstaining from any kind of sexual acting out. For a husband who has had an affair, a slip might be contacting the affair partner by phone "just to talk." A slip may be a onetime occurrence, or it may just involve serious thoughts of sliding back into old behaviors. A relapse, on the other hand, is a complete return to sinful sexual behaviors and patterns. Its intensity is determined by the possible consequences of the behaviors. In Nick's case, his choice to look at pornography at his workplace created high stakes and significant consequences—termination.

If only overt behaviors are evaluated, the potential for rebuilding trust after a slip or relapse can be destroyed. Carefully understanding and processing a slip or relapse together, however, can build trust. What happens along the path of recovery isn't always as important as what a couple can learn from it—and what can be changed in the future as a result.

Shashawna hadn't talked to me for six weeks or so, nor had she and Amani been coming for couple's counseling. Things had been going very well in their marriage, she said, and so they both had stopped working actively on their recovery. Amani had traveled out of town the previous week for business and fell into an old pattern: he allowed himself to visit a bar after his long day and began drinking and flirting with women there. By the time he found his way back to his room, it was 2:00 a.m. He and Shashawna had committed to nightly calls when he was traveling as a way to check in with each other, but on this particular evening, his call came very late and he was obviously drunk.

Shashawna was grateful that Amani had for the first time admitted that he had slipped. In the past, he would have lied about what he was doing or minimized the fact that he had consumed so much alcohol. However, she also felt angry and afraid because she knew his drinking led to promiscuous sexual acting out and she wasn't willing to live with any more affairs. "It seems it's only a matter of time," she said, "before it will happen again."

Shashawna chose not to talk to Amani that night for very long, but she asked for time to process the event when he returned. She reported that she successfully talked about her feelings and fears and her desire to have a faithful husband. He was able to hear her and share with her how he had stumbled. Months earlier, they never would have had this kind of healthy conversation.

We discussed Shashawna's need to see her husband participating in a program if he was taking his behaviors seriously. It was one of the missing pieces. She also wasn't going to delegate the scheduling of appointments to him since it was important to her that he be in therapy. She learned that she could establish bottom lines that weren't always about staying in the marriage or leaving—in this case, she just needed a commitment from Amani that he was serious about having accountability and a safe place to process his feelings. His slip was a way for her (and him) to reevaluate the path they were on. What went wrong? What changes did they need to make? When you can use slips and/or relapses as a way to learn and correct course, they can actually help strengthen trust. Of course, the slip or relapse may be simply too painful to tolerate, and you may make the more drastic decision to leave. Either way, having all of the information will lead you to the next right step.

Talking through the reasons for sinning sexually can help both you and your husband understand the underlying pain that drives unfaithful choices. If this understanding leads to changes—new boundaries, additional support, more accountability, greater awareness of original trauma—then your husband can grow as an individual, and you can as well. If the process helps you learn how to talk about difficult topics in healthy ways, you will be deepening your emotional intimacy. Even when the process is painful, you grow as you struggle together. Remember from chapter 3 that the problem is never the problem—the way you process and cope with the problem is the real problem. Trust built on a foundation of perfect behaviors with no slipups won't create emotional and spiritual connectedness in your marriage. Rather, it is the *process of building* trust that creates intimacy.

Ultimately, none of us can help making mistakes or hurting those we love. As we learn to trust ourselves to reach out for help and talk about the ways our trust has been broken, we will know intuitively when to set limits on what we will tolerate. We will discover that we can take care of ourselves if we must and that we really can control only our own behaviors and choices, not anyone else's. We'll also learn to trust the intent of our spouse's heart rather than obsessing about everything he does or doesn't do as he progresses in recovery.

Trusting God

If you are with me so far, the truth you can trust is that you cannot control your husband! No matter how hard you try, no matter how long you give it, no matter how intent you are on being a "godly" wife, only he can control his life and depend on God to enable him to be an honorable husband. The transformation may not happen on your time schedule. It may not unfold according to your plan. But you can trust God to care for his precious children—both of you.

You can trust that there is always work to do in your own life: skills to learn, confidence to develop, honesty to practice, self-care to attend to. And then you can surrender your life to God, trusting that he knows exactly what you need and when and how he will provide for you. You can trust that he sees your efforts, knows your desires, and seeks to "give you hope and a future" (Jer. 29:11). Your own process of growth may not occur as quickly as you want either, nor be as neatly packaged as you expected. Maybe you've already put in more effort than your share, taken more initiative, and been more patient than you ever imagined you could be. Your trust in God to prosper you in all circumstances is now getting tested in a concrete way that may be new to you. Will you put your trust in the only one who is really trustworthy?

Finally, you will need to trust God with your marriage. How he protects it, when he allows adversity to test it, whom he brings to support you through the struggles, what he is planning to bring to each of you as you work on it—these are mysteries at times. But if we trust that God is trustworthy, he will direct our paths (Prov. 3:6). If hurtful behaviors don't stop, you can trust God to lead you to the next right step. It may be to leave; it may be to confront; it may be to find more intensive help. You always have options.

The *American Heritage Dictionary* defines the noun *trust* as "one committed into the care of another." Perhaps we have put ourselves into the care of the wrong person as we have worked to build trust. At age twenty-one, I only knew how to trust the one who provided the deepest love I had ever experienced—my new husband, Mark. It was only through the struggle of sexual betrayal and the ensuing crises in my life that I truly began shifting my trust to God.

The crash-and-burn event in our marriage radically awakened me to my spiritual journey. I was tossed about by so many messages I had internalized about my roles in life that I really wasn't sure what was driving me. What was a "good wife" supposed to do? How did a caring mother spend her days and parent her children? What kind of career should I have to use my gifts and talents? What did success look like? How was I to serve God with my life? I was reading *When Bad Things Happen to Good People* by Harold Kushner when life as I had known it ended in my living room. I didn't believe my book selection was just coincidence. So why were these horrible things happening to us? I believed we were both good people. My spiritual journey through this adversity helped clarify my purpose: God was going to grow me up and lead me to depend on and serve him in ways I had never known before.

Is it possible that God gave me the great task of struggling with trust so that I would put my trust in him *first*, before expanding it to other relationships? I think that is much of what my journey through sexual betrayal has been about. If I'd never had to work at trusting, I would have forever been comfortable trusting my husband for everything I needed. I never would have stretched to really understand the words that I so often read and heard: "Trust in the LORD with all your heart and lean not on your own understanding; in all your ways submit to him, and he will make your paths straight" (Prov. 3:5–6).

When you put your trust in your heavenly Father, he will meet your heart's deepest needs, even when your earthly relationships cannot. He may not do it in the way you expect, but in his timing and with his guidance, you will be given the people, resources, and experiences you need to survive and to keep growing. Developing the capacity to trust deeply is much more involved than simply growing to trust your husband's sexual behaviors. It's about totally trusting God so that you can release your fears and anxieties about other people and activities in your life, knowing that *you will be all right* no matter what happens outside of you.

Affirming What Is Good

Mark was a poster child for remorse and brokenness after his intervention. He was truly repentant and intent on being a new man. He participated in his recovery program faithfully; he sought to be an accountable, trustworthy person each day. He was patient with my feelings, and he was willing to do whatever it took to stay sexually sober and to assure me that he was. But I didn't always appreciate the good changes that were occurring because I was still releasing my feelings of anger, fear, sadness, and confusion.

In fact, my antennae were up and searching for any little thing that would validate my point or justify my current feeling. I could find some things for sure: "You took twenty minutes longer than necessary to drive the babysitter home." "You forgot to tell me about your trip next week." "That woman hugged you too tightly at the conference." We learned to talk about each of these events, and slowly I began to trust the intent of Mark's heart to be a godly husband and father.

If both you and your husband are committed to building trust with each other and are taking steps to do so, then I encourage you to notice and affirm what is *good* in your trust-building process. It's so easy to find the flaws, to point out the mistakes, to overreact to the imperfections. Building trust is about making changes. And the change process involves times of chaos as you practice incorporating new behaviors. Making a change is never a neatly orchestrated operation. You must go through periods of confusion, frustration, risk, and practice before you learn something new. The process takes great patience and perseverance. While you work on building a new kind of trust in your life, you'll find it helpful to follow the advice Paul gave the Philippians: "Whatever is true, whatever is noble, whatever is right, whatever is pure, whatever is lovely, whatever is admirable—if anything is excellent or praiseworthy—think about such things" (Phil. 4:8). You have a choice to look for behaviors that are changing for the better or to focus on everything that is going wrong.

The kind of trust that will be a worthy companion for a lifetime allows you to *live in the moment*—to enjoy what you can about today and your relationship where it is right now—without looking back and without looking forward. You will know you are learning to trust when you can begin to live like that.

Thinking It Over

1. Did you trust your husband unconditionally when you first married? How have you handled minor trust breaks?

2. Who else in your life has broken your trust?

3. Can you identify ways your husband is working at being trustworthy?

4. How are you working to trust yourself?

5. In what specific ways is God protecting, providing, and leading you through the pain and complexities of sexual betrayal?

CHAPTER 8

Is Forgiving Him Really Possible?

It's Easier and Harder Than You Think

The old law of an eye for an eye leaves everybody blind.
Martin Luther King Jr.

Get rid of all bitterness, rage and anger, brawling and slander, along with every form of malice. Be kind and compassionate to one another, forgiving each other, just as in Christ God forgave you.
Ephesians 4:31–32

One of the most difficult challenges of the journey through the pain of sexual betrayal is getting rid of anger, resentment, and bitterness. Shedding pounds when we're on a weight reduction program is not unlike shedding the weight of burdensome emotions after we have been betrayed. The process is not a quick one—at least not if it is authentic and lasting. You can't *quickly* forgive your husband of sinful sexual choices that have damaged lifelong memories and trust and then hope everything will be all right. Forgiveness just doesn't work that way.

Tim came in for a counseling session with his wife, Jenna, to finally disclose to her the full nature of his sexual acting out. It included years of pornography, visits to massage parlors, and several affairs. He rattled through his list of offenses rather emotionlessly, then said, "Jenna, I'm asking you to forgive me. Will you forgive me?" When she couldn't force herself to blurt out the answer he wanted, he leaned forward and reminded her that, biblically, she needed to do so. He even quoted Scripture: "And when you stand praying, if you hold anything against anyone, forgive them, so that your Father in heaven may forgive you your sins" (Mark 11:25).

Jenna started weeping quietly and said, "I'm going to need some time."

Tim was clearly irritated and angry that his wife hadn't "obeyed" — in his mind, she wasn't being a good Christian woman. His pressure on her to forgive him continued; and in fact, so did his acting out. The two of them argued about forgiving and forgetting the past for many months to come. Tim insisted that Jenna had her own sins that she needed to disclose and deal with, and he wouldn't focus on his behaviors seriously until she did. It's common for a man like Tim who just doesn't get it — who hasn't been broken by his betrayal and isn't owning the wrongs he has done — to excuse himself and blame his wife for the sinful choices he made. When a wife is under regular attack, she doesn't have much time to figure out her own losses, feelings, behavior patterns, or anything else; she tends to use all of her energy to protect herself from further pain. Because Tim was so invested in blaming Jenna and demanding that she adhere to his interpretation of biblical obedience, his anger never subsided and Jenna's pain and anger were never heard. They divorced several months later.

For me, forgiveness was a slow process that involved moving through a series of steps. The thought of saying anything hurriedly to Mark never even crossed my mind. "I forgive you, dear," didn't pop out of my mouth in those first months. (But a lot of other things did!) The process of focusing on myself and my own imperfections is what led me beyond judgment to compassion. I'm sure some people feel called to be more official with statements of forgiveness; my style was to *show* forgiveness by becoming a woman who behaved in forgiving ways. Whatever your style, I encourage you to make your forgiveness authentic and lasting. If words come easily but consistency does not, practicing living out your forgiveness one day at a time may be more congruent with your heart's desire to forgive. You'll know if it's working, because over time you will be released from the bondage of bitterness and resentment.

Fortunately, Mark was so broken by his behaviors and consequences that he had no expectations of me to forgive him. He never pressured me to say something to him. He never asked me to forget about the past. I experienced great losses, and I had a great deal of anger and pain to process before I was ready to forgive authentically. I needed time to walk through the stages of grieving before I could do anything.

A few years ago I came across a book that described and validated the journey toward forgiveness better than anything else I have ever read or heard. The premise of R. T. Kendall's book *Total Forgiveness* is that forgiveness isn't a simple assignment of "signing off" on someone's behaviors.[1] It isn't about forgetting the past and moving on, nor is it necessarily about reconciliation. It is a process that requires a heart change. As you forgive the one who betrayed you, you will find yourself talking differently about him, thinking differently about him, and extending mercy to him. This kind of forgiveness invites you into the process *yourself*, recognizing that you can extend true forgiveness only if you have been on the receiving end of it.

Misconceptions about Forgiveness

You may avoid or delay forgiving your husband because you perceive that forgiveness means you must do some things that feel anything but authentic to you. In *Total Forgiveness*, Kendall lists several common misconceptions about forgiveness. Understanding what it is *not* can be a critical step toward living it out in a relationship damaged by sexual betrayal.

Extending forgiveness to your husband doesn't mean you must *approve* of what he did. Part of my journey involved getting educated about addiction, the roots of the behaviors, and the motivation behind Mark's sinful choices. As I learned the "why" behind his behaviors, I became more accepting. I also came to believe that his choices really weren't about *me*. But even with that information, I didn't have to approve of his choices. Neither did I need to *excuse* or *justify* what he did. Forgiveness has nothing to do with making right what was wrong.

To forgive your husband, you don't need to release him from the consequences of his behavior—in other words, you don't need to *pardon* him. Mark's sexual acting out threatened the financial stability of our family. Lawsuits were pending, and the potential of losing everything loomed large. I needed to protect myself and the kids, and I did so by establishing bank accounts in my name and the children's names and separating other financial assets for a time. Even though Mark was crushed by the thought of dividing our finances, I didn't need to pardon him from that consequence. It was a natural outcome of his past behavior.

You may feel compelled to pardon any number of other natural consequences, but extending forgiveness doesn't mean you are obligated to protect your husband from the costs of his actions. Some men distance themselves from family members, refusing to talk about their sin. To keep the peace in the family, you may feel you should keep the lines of communication open or go out of your way to arrange visits with family members. But you are not responsible for keeping everyone connected and informed, especially if you are covering up the truth in the process.

You also don't need to *deny* your husband's betrayal. You aren't required to hide the truth for the sake of keeping the peace. You don't need to act as if everything is fine when it really isn't. Nor are you asked to *forget* the betrayal. You can't possibly forget significant events, whether positive or negative, that have happened in your life unless you have become an expert at disassociation. Moreover, you don't develop emotional health by trying to erase unwanted memories from your mind. There is no healthy way to blot out life-changing events. You must learn how to integrate the feelings created from them and grow through them. Out of your wounds, you can minister to others. If you just forget your pain, you can't be an agent of godly change. Don't let anyone convince you that you must "forgive and forget." Authentic forgiveness requires you to accept your feelings and make conscious decisions in the midst of them.

Kendall also points out that forgiveness doesn't mean you *refuse* to take the wrong seriously. You don't need to minimize the severity of sexual sin. Just because many others may be doing it, or your husband didn't realize how easily he could be lured into unhealthy choices, or he was unaware of the power of his own abusive history, doesn't mean his sexual acting out is not very serious.

One of the greatest fears wives have regarding forgiveness is that they will have to *relinquish* any further feelings of hurt or anger if they choose to forgive. You may think that "from forgiveness on" you must pretend that you no longer feel hurt. Shelly told Steve that she forgave him for an affair he had when their first child was born. "While I never blame him for the affair today or ever mention it to anyone else," Shelly told me, "I feel sad and lonely when I see him spending time with a woman — like at our neighborhood picnic. When I've tried to share my feelings and the triggers that situations like that create for me, he gets impatient and angry with me and says, 'I thought you said you forgave me for that affair. You obviously didn't mean it.'" Authentic forgiveness doesn't mean you must surrender your feelings!

Furthermore, total forgiveness doesn't necessarily require you to *reconcile* with your husband. You may believe that if you choose to forgive, then you must choose to reconcile as well. But these are two separate decisions. Sometimes you don't even have a choice to reconcile. Your husband may be the one who has decided to leave *you*, despite his choices of infidelity. Or perhaps he has elected not to get help and continues making unhealthy decisions that dishonor your relationship. You don't need to let people hurt you; safe boundaries may require separation from your husband.

Finally, remember that *forgiveness* is not synonymous with *trust*. Just because you have forgiven your husband for unfaithfulness, doesn't mean you need to be ready to trust him again. These are two separate issues. Linda's spouse confronted her with these words: "You just told me that you forgave me for the affairs I had last year, so why don't you trust me? You must not have meant what you said." Actually, she *did* mean what she said! His job is to begin the process of becoming a trustworthy man. You can forgive but still have reservations about trust.

If you are feeling hurt and bitter, are you having difficulty believing that you will ever be able to forgive? Maybe you wonder if you are being *too* compassionate and accommodating to your husband and neglecting your own afflicted feelings. I encourage you to take your time in the forgiveness process. God wants your forgiveness to be authentic, and the beginning of your process may involve just a vision to forgive some day. Don't feel pressured to hurry. If you are working on your own healing, forgiveness will come in time.

The Truth about Forgiveness

After examining what forgiveness is *not*, Kendall explains what it *is*. Before you can even consider forgiving someone, you need to know *what* you are forgiving. The concept seems ridiculously elementary, yet many women get stuck here at the first step because their husband denies them the total disclosure of his betrayal. They long to move forward in the healing process, but they know intuitively that they don't know what they need to know: *everything*.

Mark acted out with another woman for the first time relatively early on in our marriage — perhaps the fourth year or so. Although he had struggled with masturbation and pornography since he was twelve, he hadn't crossed the "flesh line" until this time. He remorsefully went to a supervising pastor to confess his actions. He was reaching out for guidance, taking the opportunity to come clean, seek help, and make changes. In the readiness of that moment to live life differently, he was advised to cover up his sexual sin: "Mark, don't mention anything about your behavior to Deb—it will just hurt her. And don't ever do it again." Consequently, there was no confession, no repentance, no regret, and no opportunity for me to know the truth (consciously at least). Early in our marriage we were robbed of the opportunity to experience brokenness, surrender, and forgiveness. The next ten years might have been very different if the facts had been out and the process of forgiving and healing could have begun.

When I encourage total disclosure between couples, the most important motivation is to provide the sacred ground for forgiveness and trust building to take place. If you seek facts, do so for the sake of forgiving. When your husband offers you the facts of his betrayal, he is essentially handing over a nuclear weapon. His disclosure is an extremely vulnerable decision. You now hold the power to do very damaging warfare—to other people and to your marriage. If your anger and bitterness are out of control, then perhaps you're not worthy of the power with which you have been entrusted. Be advised that you are being called to enter a holy place of healing. You have a choice to destroy or to learn mercy.

Authentic forgiveness means *choosing to keep no record of wrongs* (1 Cor. 13:5). Can you grasp what is being asked of you here? Keeping no record of your husband's offenses means you must stop keeping score. You must stop evaluating who has done worse things in your marriage and who is the worse spouse. You must stop case building—finding example after example from the past to prove your point today. It means you must let go of the "life sentence" you may feel compelled to hang on to. Even more, it means you must drop any labels you have been giving each other: addict, coaddict, codependent, overreactive wife, abusive husband,

and so on. We are men and women. We've all made mistakes; we all fall short; we all struggle. And we all need to be reconciled to God through his Son, Jesus Christ, for alone, we have no hope to save ourselves.

Kevin has been participating dutifully in his recovery program, confessing his wrongs, finding other men to hold him accountable for his sexual choices, and sharing his feelings, needs, and desires with his wife. Yet Jessica can't seem to let go of the past. She announced in group, "Kevin's addict keeps withdrawing and hiding, and it is so hurtful to me." Her description of her husband as an addict, though, had nothing to do with the fact that he was withdrawing. Many people withdraw — some with addictions and some without. The truth was that Kevin was feeling something, perhaps fear or sadness, and was coping by withdrawing. In contrast, Jessica was coping with her hurt by being critical. Labels and generalizations don't help us find understanding and empathy.

If you are working at forgiving, you will *refuse to punish* your husband for his behaviors. We can punish others in either passive-aggressive ways or direct ways. Sarcasm is one of the subtle forms of punishment that is hard to control and easily used because it is received with laughter. If you still feel anger toward your husband but don't want others to know, you can cover it up with humor — and it comes out as sarcasm.

Carla was in the church lobby visiting with friends when her husband came up and complimented her on how nice she looked. She turned to her friends and said, "Yes, my husband is an expert at picking up pretty women!" The Latin root of *sarcasm* means "to tear the flesh"; Carla's sarcastic comment tore the flesh of her husband, who previously had wounded her with his infidelity but today was trying to honor her.

Beth decided to start spending money carelessly, subconsciously getting back at her husband, who had used family money to procure prostitutes. She was outraged that she had sacrificed for years to make the family budget work, and she hadn't yet found a healthy way to express her anger.

Another aspect of forgiveness is to *use discretion* in sharing facts of the sexual betrayal with others. Don't gossip for the sake of spreading the news to anyone and everyone. Don't relieve yourself of pain by spewing out the hurt to whomever happens to be listening. Guard the reputation of your husband even though he has hurt you. Instead of talking indiscriminately about the wrongs your husband has committed, find several safe women who will hear your whole story and support you. We all need to have safe people and places to talk about our pain, and it *is* possible to talk with discretion.

As I was working through some of the roadblocks to writing this book, I realized one of them had to do with this dimension of forgiveness: I wanted to guard Mark's reputation and the truth about who he is—a very good man. By sharing my story of pain and redemption, I knew it would be necessary to share some of Mark's sinful sexual choices. I wasn't convinced I wanted to do that—to drag out bits and pieces of our painful past. When I talked with Mark about my dilemma, he thanked me for being sensitive, then assured me that nothing I would write would differ from what he already shares when he tells his story through his writing and speaking. Only with his complete blessing did I agree to write a book for women.

Another aspect of forgiveness is to *be merciful*. Kendall reminds us that receiving mercy means *not* getting something we *do* deserve; mercy differs from grace, which means *getting* something we *don't* deserve. If you extend mercy to your husband, you are withholding revenge for the hurt he has caused you. You make a decision not to get even—not to give him what he deserves. You offer mercy by withholding your justice for his betrayal. A decision to be merciful is a decision to turn justice over to God. If he decides that justice must be rendered, then he will provide the circumstances. Wanting things to be fair—today—is an urgency that is hard to let go. Most of us are so impatient that we can't imagine waiting months, years, or even a lifetime for God's justice. And the truth is that we may not even witness justice in our lifetime. We aren't given that guarantee. In fact, God may decide to extend mercy to your husband, just as he often extends mercy to you and me for our sins.

Tonya confessed to me that she was explosively angry when her husband admitted to having an affair. "Anton knew how devastated I would be because we had talked about the pain I felt watching my father cheat on my mother. I couldn't believe what I was hearing when he finally admitted his secret relationship. I didn't even call a friend or let any of the pain sink in before I called an old boyfriend and invited him to be sexual with me." Tonya took justice into her own hands. She was intent on showing him what betrayal felt like. Working to forgive means we are willing to *give up getting even* in some way.

When you decide to forgive, you work to *be gracious* in the process, says Kendall. You have many opportunities to tell the truth—the whole truth. Being gracious is about choosing what you don't say when you could be saying more. This element of forgiveness is tricky, because I've been challenging you to practice being authentic. But I believe that being authentic first involves discerning when it is safe to do so. Not all people can be trusted with all confidences; you must decide the kind of company you are keeping! If you're in safe company, you can decide how brutally honest you will be versus how generally authentic you will be. The choice is not black-and-white—to tell everything or to tell nothing.

Recently when I visited with my father-in-law, who lives in a nursing home, he asked me how Mark was doing and what he was speaking about these days. I wanted to be honest about the healing influence Mark was having on many hurting people. However, Mark and I had agreed previously that we didn't want to divulge the nature of his speeches, which sometimes exposed the abuse his father had perpetrated. I chose to be gracious but authentic: "Dad, you would be proud of Mark and all he is doing for people hurting from sexual sin. He speaks from his heart with great compassion."

True forgiveness is a choice from the heart. It is not an agenda item to get through. It is a decision you make when you trust your heart enough to know you are ready. Only you will know when you have healed enough so that you will no longer choose to punish, keep score, uncover more facts, spread gossip, or judge your husband.

Total forgiveness, Kendall says, also means that you may have to *forgive God*—in other words, release the bitterness you feel toward God. If you believe God is omniscient, omnipresent, and omnipotent, you may wonder how he could allow such horrible things to happen to you. Why didn't he, in his power, stop your husband's terrible choices? After all, God loves marriage and faithfulness. In your efforts to find healing, you must confront any anger and bitterness you feel because a gracious God has allowed you to suffer.

After the disclosure of Mark's betrayal, I was very angry with God. I thought I had sacrificed every fiber of my being to be a good wife and mother. "Why me?" I wondered. "Am I such a disappointment to God that he has turned away from watching over my life?" Years later, when I could more clearly see purpose in my suffering, I was able to let go of my anger at God for not sparing me from the painful events and adversity in my life.

Finally, total forgiveness means you need to *forgive yourself.* I'm not sure this paragraph belongs last, because I now know that in working to forgive myself, I've become much more aware of how to forgive others. I was awakened to my own brokenness as I muddled through the pain of betrayal. I, too, had hurt people and damaged relationships. I, too, minimized the truths about who I am in Christ. In not believing that I was adequate, lovable, cared about, and chosen, I coped in unhealthy and hurtful ways. I wasn't all that I could be—all that God created me to be.

Kendall speaks pointedly to some of us when he writes, "Probably what we all want to say is, 'Well, what I did wasn't nearly as bad as what they have done!' And that's where we are wrong! God hates self-righteousness as much as he hates the injustice that you think is so horrible, and He certainly doesn't like it when we judge. So if you must forget the sins of which God has forgiven you, at least remember that one of the most heinous sins of all is self-righteousness."[2] Stepping down from my self-righteous perch and owning what I do (and what I neglect to do) allows God to change my character.

I couldn't begin to know how to forgive Mark completely if I didn't first experience forgiveness for myself. And I needed to know what I was forgiving myself for before I could do it! I wouldn't have known to examine my life if I hadn't been in enough pain to do so. Therefore, this *process* of forgiveness was what most enlightened me to a major purpose of my pain — to make me capable of being a broken companion to others, especially my husband, as we explore and forgive how we have silently and secretly tried to manage our lives in ineffective and harmful ways.

Thinking It Over

1. Are you ready to consider forgiving your husband? What are your fears about doing so?

2. What, specifically, are you forgiving?

3. Are you able to work at forgiving your husband without completely trusting him or making a decision about reconciliation? Why or why not?

4. If you haven't forgiven God for allowing sexual betrayal to harm your marriage, how might you begin this process?

5. For what do you feel you need to forgive yourself? Is something specific stopping you from being able to do so?

CHAPTER 9

How Can We Rebuild Our Relationship?

Creating a Shared Vision for a Passionate Alliance

Choose thy love; love thy choice.

Anonymous

Two are better than one, because they have a good return for their labor: If they fall down, they can help each other up.

Ecclesiastes 4:9–10

Recently I woke up surprised by a dream I'd had: I dreamed I was alone. After more than thirty years of choosing to stay in my marriage and recover from sexual betrayal, I couldn't figure out what would prompt me to have such a dream.

I've been writing for months now about my healing journey—from shattered dreams to renewed vision. Chapter after chapter, I've discussed my need to focus on *me*, the changes I wanted to make, and the lessons God was teaching me through my pain. These chapters have been about letting go of thinking that someone else was responsible to provide me with safety, passion, and worth.

I think my dream was a reminder that I needed to be all right alone, even if I was in a loving relationship. I was not to *lose myself* by failing to take the time to know myself, to grow, and to create a vision for my life. Even if my husband and I created a shared vision, I was not to let go of my personal vision. Prior to my heal-ing journey, I expected that my marriage would provide me with everything I needed to be completely satisfied and happy in life. In essence, I had divorced myself by giving Mark all of the power to make my life happy.

Now my vision for our relationship is built on my *desires*, not on my *needs*. I don't *need* to build a vision with my husband; I *want* to. This kind of loving alliance should be the aim of any mature relationship: "I don't need you; I want you." When you can think about your marriage in this way, you're ready to design an authen-tic vision for you and your husband as a couple.

Replacing the Old with the New

One spring Mark and I decided to repair our back porch. It had some weak spots where the wood was rotting, and Mark thought a few replacement boards would take care of the problem. As he began tearing out the worst of the boards, we could see that weather had weakened the frame as well. Before long, our project left us standing on bare ground; we'd had to remove the entire structure! With tired eyes, he gazed at me and said, "This reminds me of our journey. We had to completely tear out the damaged, weakened parts of our marriage, and now it's time to rebuild."

In the early months and years of healing from sexual betrayal, the bulk of your recovery efforts may be devoted to damage con-trol. It's no fun stepping around on weakened boards wondering if or when you're going to fall through. If you don't replace the boards, you'll soon decide you'd rather not step out on the porch at all. It's time to replace the old with new. If you've been working hard to remove betrayal, secrets, coping behaviors, and expecta-tions, then you are ready to create a vision together. When I first learned of Mark's, betrayal, I was tempted to think I just wanted to go back to the life we had. Parts of it were very good and satisfying. But we had so much more to experience as we transformed our relationship—building something altogether new. Building a vision for your relationship is an intentional process, and as with any new building venture, the process is energized by passion and connection.

As God leads you through the steps of healing from the pain of sexual betrayal, he won't waste the efforts you've put forth to understand your life and that of your husband. He will use this crisis to give you an opportunity to delve more deeply into each other's stories—the experiences of your past that formed the person you are today. God will use the character growth that you have been cultivating and the new information that you have gathered to prepare you for a richer, more intimate relationship. Your pain has served to grow you up in many ways. You are wiser, more mature, and more capable of having a deep emotional and spiritual connection.

Mark and I began creating a new vision together by symbolically starting again—renewing our marriage vows. We chose a new date to celebrate our new beginning. Like a newly engaged couple, we shopped together for rings and then invited several recovery friends to share in our ceremony. Exchanging personally written vows and new rings, we rededicated ourselves to God's purpose, plan, and vision for our marriage—our one-flesh union.

We had passed through a stage of trying to be everything to each other. We thought that agreeing on everything was vision. And then we'd entered a stage of living two very separate lives, creating a personal vision but not a shared vision. Some husbands and wives are guided by personal visions but fail to work on a shared vision, thus creating *di-vision*. Having both a personal vision and a couple's vision is vital to a healthy relationship.

To work on a vision as a couple, we need to be on the same side—allies, so to speak. We need to let go of the temptation to think, "I'm right and you're wrong," "My ideas are better than yours," "I'm more important than you are," "My talents are more valuable than yours," and so on. As allies, we are interested in combining our strengths and weaknesses. We accept that together we are much more than either of us is alone. If my vision is to be like my spouse or to make my spouse be like me, then one of us would be irrelevant! God brought two people together with two very different sets of skills and temperaments so that together they would be greater than either one alone.

How Couples Develop

As I was sorting out how to make sense of what happened in our marriage, I felt empowered after I learned how couples develop. This knowledge led me to some important insights about myself. It also helped me determine where Mark and I got stuck as a couple as we tried to grow closer but sometimes fell away from each other instead.

In their book *In Quest of the Mythical Mate*, Drs. Ellyn Bader and Peter Pearson describe the five stages of a couple's development: enmeshment, differentiation, practicing, reengagement, and mutual interdependence.[1] According to Bader and Pearson, couples grow and develop in much the same way a child develops. Just as a child must navigate through stages to develop healthy skills to grow and thrive, so must our relationship navigate through these stages to grow and thrive. Each stage requires couples to master specific tasks, and each stage is more complex than the one before. Often distance between two people in a relationship is created when one or both are unable to develop the skills necessary to move to the next stage of development. As we look more closely at the tasks that are accomplished in each stage of development, we can then see where we might be stuck—individually and as a couple.

Enmeshment

The first stage of couple development is *enmeshment*. In this stage of infatuation, individuals are like heat-seeking missiles. Intense bonding occurs. During enmeshment, you fall madly in love and never have enough time to do all of the talking and sharing you desire. Rarely do you notice that you have differences—in fact, you focus almost exclusively on your similarities. It is a period of temporary insanity—you will go to any lengths to please your partner. In this stage you don't have any interest in changing each other. Your needs seem to be nurtured completely by each other and you feel unconditionally accepted and loved. Also in this stage you begin to trust each other unconditionally, even though you haven't known each other very long. The ultimate purpose of this stage is attachment—to become a couple.

For most of us, this stage is hard to forget. We built dreams of our marriage during this time. Movies and magazines validate this enmeshed kind of love, and for a time, we think we've found the promised land of relationship. We think we'll be satisfied forever and will never have unmet needs again. We have found our soul mate—the one who will make us eternally happy.

I remember when Mark and I were engaged, dreaming about the day when we would finally live together. I specifically recall telling Mark that it didn't matter where we lived; I would be happy as long as we were together. Just eighteen months later, we moved from the quaint university town of Princeton, New Jersey, to the cornfields of Iowa, and I was miserable! While we were in the enmeshment stage of our relationship, I liked any idea Mark had or any plan he proposed for us. Now that we were moving into the next stage of our couple development, I realized I didn't always agree with his tastes or decisions.

During enmeshment, you look for the best in each other and deny that you have differences at times. This stage is about forging a strong attachment between the two of you.

Differentiation

No sooner do we settle into our newfound wonderland than the next stage of couple development arrives: *differentiation*. In this stage, reality hits and differences begin to emerge. You realize that you have diverse feelings and thoughts and that you need to stand out as a unique individual. You notice things about your mate that take you by surprise. No longer do you love everything about each other! During this stage, you remove each other from the unrealistic pedestal created during enmeshment. And you begin to feel guilt and fear, wondering why you don't feel the same as you did in the enmeshment stage. Because the high of enmeshment has worn off, some people in this stage decide they've married the wrong person and leave the relationship; the appearance of so many differences is too unsettling for them. Others feel overwhelmed by the changes in this stage and confused by the shift; they might turn to coping mechanisms to medicate any feelings that aren't discussed in healthy ways — feelings such as disillusionment, loneliness, fear, or anger.

I realized soon after we were married that Mark liked to stay up late and watch TV before going to bed; I preferred to go to bed earlier, read, and get up early in the morning. He loved to have a lot of people around; I was content being alone. He liked to eat early; I liked to eat later. He enjoyed destressing with television; I hated to sit still. Differences between us cropped up everywhere, and my feelings about them became more intense. In those early years of marriage, we weren't equipped to engage in meaningful conversation about our differences, so each of us coped in our own way to manage our unspoken feelings.

Practicing

After the differentiation stage, a couple will move on to *practicing*. In this stage, you each practice being a unique individual, developing your self-esteem and self-worth within your relationship. Practically, you may be growing your career or starting a family, and so your focus is on your individual needs. You are not as interested in nurturing the relationship as you are in growing your individual identity. You need more time alone and actually pull away from spending a lot of time together. To negotiate this stage, you need to find your own voice, which requires you to identify and express your feelings, needs, thoughts, and desires. If you are being authentic, you don't hide (or cope with) your internal processes. You share honestly what is going on inside of you. This stage is very difficult, often involving conflict as couples move away from each other to work on their personal development.

Religious or family messages may prevent you from entering the practicing stage. If your only job as a "good Christian wife" is to please your husband, or if you haven't been allowed to have needs of your own, thinking about yourself and concentrating on your needs may feel selfish. A time will come to refocus on serving each other, but it's essential to mature in your relationship by developing who you are as an individual *within* your relationship. If you've ever felt as though you were losing yourself, you may have sacrificed all of your feelings, needs, and desires to tend to your husband and others.

You must be able to solve conflict in a healthy way to continue to grow as a couple. As I mentioned, the practicing stage creates great change in your relationship as you and your husband put distance between each other. Where once you were caring intensely for each other's needs, now you are pulling away to focus inward. Feelings of abandonment and rejection can emerge, necessitating some difficult conversations. How are you at dealing with anger and resentment? What do you do or how do you talk when these feelings surface? If you don't like confrontation or don't know how to have healthy conversations, you won't be prepared to move to the next developmental stage.

The practicing stage is also a time when a personal vision can become more established within the context of marriage. For many couples, this idea seems foreign. But if you neglect your own passions and needs, you will set yourself up to be disappointed in your relationship. By working on an individual plan for emotional, physical, sexual, social, and spiritual health, you can let go of the expectation that your husband must take care of all of your needs. Your husband can't be everything for you, nor you for him.

Reengagement

The fourth stage of couple development is *reengagement*, a time of coming and going. After establishing your personal identity, you become more available again to be vulnerable in the relationship. You don't fear losing yourself as you did in the earlier stages. You enjoy intimate connection as well as times apart. When tension arises regarding the ways you spend your time, you are more skilled at resolving conflict. You begin to see how the triggers in your relationship awaken the pain of the past.

Mark and I both traveled frequently for our careers. When we were apart, we worked on a personal vision: how we would strengthen our spiritual life alone, what kind of work we would do on our own, how we would parent alone, what our social life would look like when we were alone, how we would handle financial matters by ourselves, and so on. When both of us were home, we changed gears to include each other in spiritual growth, work, parenting, socializing, and finances. But even when we were together, we learned not to neglect aspects of our lives as individuals.

The challenge is to have passion and plans for your personal life as well as for your marriage. Whether you are alone or with your husband, you can find pleasure and purpose in your life so that you don't perpetuate an unhealthy enmeshment.

Mutual Interdependence

In the final stage, *mutual interdependence*, you experience constancy in your relationship. With each of you confident and satisfied in your own identity, your relationship is built on *growth*, not *need*. You have found a bond of love that is deep and satisfying, and you can accept the realness of your relationship while letting go of your need for it to be perfect. At this stage, your relationship reflects authenticity and intimacy: it's okay to feel; it's okay to have conflict; it's okay to have needs; it's safe to commit; it's safe to be vulnerable.

Each stage presents a couple with the issue of how to manage *closeness* and *distance*. In *enmeshment*, a couple seeks closeness at all times and avoids distancing. In *differentiation*, the couple continues to be close, but each partner starts desiring some distance. In *practicing*, the couple practices intentional distancing, and husband and wife don't feel as close. In *reengagement*, a couple is sporadically close and distant, learning to negotiate and balance the two ends of the spectrum. Finally, in *mutual interdependence*, the couple experiences closeness and distance, but the shift between the two is more fluid, expected, and constant. In this last stage, individuals can be alone but not feel lonely.

I found it helpful to be able to identify what stage Mark and I were working on as a couple. Awareness of each stage helped to normalize what was going on in our relationship and helped us not to feel as though we were hopeless or falling apart or not meant for each other. Every couple passes through these stages if both husband and wife are committed to growing together. I have said and heard others say as well, "I long to have something *more* in my marriage." When I studied this process, I saw much more clearly how I wanted to grow personally *and* as a couple.

In the early years of marriage, I was scared to think we were growing apart. Although there were many practical reasons for the increasing distance between us (jobs, children, buying a home), I thought the state of being madly in love was supposed to last forever. When I longed to have time to pursue more of my own interests and talents, I felt guilty, thinking I should only want to be with my husband. When Mark became more engaged in his demanding career, I quickly felt left out and unimportant; I had just as much difficulty letting him pursue his unique, individual life.

When crisis hit our marriage, we were still figuring out the differentiation stage. We had only dabbled in the practicing stage; we didn't know how to talk about the feelings we had about our differences, and we usually found it easiest to live separate lives while sharing a house and kids. I ached for the "more" in my life that I didn't even know how to describe. Now I know I longed for mutual interdependence in my marriage. I needed to know that we both could feel confident about ourselves and that we were choosing the relationship not out of need but out of the desire to be together.

Forging a Healthy Alliance

When Mark and I married, we were enmeshed—no doubt about it! We had much to learn to enjoy the kind of marriage I dreamed about. I had no idea so much work would be involved in growing a mature relationship. I've heard people say you shouldn't get married until you have completed yourself—then you will be more likely to be happy. The truth is, a committed relationship is the place where we figure out how to manage closeness and distance without losing ourselves or losing the ones we love. It is a graduate-level course, and you can't do the coursework alone.

In *Sacred Marriage*, Gary Thomas articulately expresses the journey I knew I wanted to be on:

> Since there is so much immorality within us—not just lust, but selfishness, anger, control-mongering, and even hatred—we should enter into a close relationship with one other person so we can work on those issues in the light of what our marriage relationship will reveal to us about our behavior and our attitudes. I found there was a tremendous amount of immaturity [and woundedness] within me that my marriage directly

confronted. The key was that I had to change my view of marriage. If the purpose of marriage was simply to enjoy an infatuation and make me "happy," then I'd have to get a "new" marriage every two or three years. But if I really wanted to see God transform me from the inside out, I'd need to concentrate on changing *myself* rather than on changing my *spouse*.[2]

What makes you allies, anyway? How do you become companions and teammates? Look at the chart below and identify which characteristics apply to you:

Enemy or Ally?

Characteristics of Enemies	Characteristics of Allies
Think their spouse is the enemy (problem)	Think they work as a team
Someone wins/someone loses	The goal is win/win
Manipulation	Cooperation
Controlling	Supportive, affirming, encouraging
Self-centered attitude — believe their needs are most important	There is a common vision
Conflicting values	Tolerance, patience
Critical	Empathetic
Seek power	Accommodate differences
Exploit each others' weaknesses	Admit weaknesses and vulnerabilities
Attack/Blame each other	Combine strengths
Motivated by self-preservation, fear, pride, anger, shame, victimization	Teachable — not afraid to learn or change
Lead lives of isolation	Lead lives as companions — desire to be together

When you think about your marriage, do any of these characteristics describe your relationship? Are you working as enemies or allies most of the time? This chart is not a measure of good or bad, right or wrong. Rather, it is intended to lay out some specific tools that will help you work to be better companions. Remember, you can always begin to work on your "ally" characteristics whether your husband chooses to or not. The dynamics of a team will change as each player does.

Jennifer sent me an email describing the shift in her relationship with her husband:

> I realized that my recovery has been like being on a team. In our couple's therapy session, you and Mark talked to us about being allies or enemies, and although I feel like Chad and I have been on the same team, the nature of my team has changed since being in recovery.
>
> Before recovery, I was definitely the captain of the team. I was first. I would say that God was second on the team, and if ever I thought I needed help with anything, I would ask him what he thought. Chad was somewhere down there in the roster, maybe third or even lower. In fact, when he would screw up, I would try to figure out what he needed to do, or I might decide he needed to get kicked off the team for a while! Sometimes I would ask God what to do with him (or the kids), and then I would try to fix them.
>
> But now I feel like our team is very different. The number one player on our team is God for sure. And Chad and I are second in line. But I no longer try to decide what to do for everyone on the team. If things aren't going right, Chad and I go to God and wait for him to tell us what to do. We are definitely allies and teammates—no one is more important than the other.

Jennifer had been betrayed by years of pornography and sexual affairs, so my heart warmed to hear her describe the victory of being allies. No amount of betrayal or pain needs to prevent you from walking through the steps of self-examination, brokenness, surrender, forgiveness, and trust so that you can emerge ready to be a teammate. If you have decided that you can be an ally, you are ready to put back into your life joyful and purposeful activities to replace the things you've worked hard to get out—secrets, isolation, and harmful coping behaviors. When you can do that, you'll be playing in the major leagues.

Creating a Shared Vision

A vision is a clear mental picture of where we desire to go in the future. It arises out of our perception of God's calling, plan, and purpose for our life. When we develop this vision, it will help us make daily decisions based on their consistency with the vision.

Mark and I felt God's calling on our lives to work together, ministering to couples who were dealing with sexual addiction. As our vision grew, we began looking for a physical space in which to do this work. We soon began noticing For Sale signs and, ultimately, a building site that is now home to our counseling center. With the vision of working together planted firmly in our minds, we began seeing possibilities we never would have noticed before.

Creating a shared vision keeps you on track when the going gets tough. And the going will get tough. Having a vision for the future requires making changes in the present—and change always brings with it loss, chaos, and mixed emotions. Even if the change you seek is good, you leave something behind as you move on to a new challenge. When you work together to create a shared vision, you experience not only joy in building something new, but also sadness in letting go of something familiar. Learning to talk about those feelings together is another way you connect emotionally as a couple.

A shared vision should encompass every area of your life together. However, since you can't tackle everything at once, allow me to suggest five key areas to focus on as a starting place: emotional health, work, social life, sexuality, and spiritual life.

Emotional Health

Having a vision for emotional health as a couple might include deciding how you want to manage out-of-control feelings, conflict, or "stuck places" in your relationship. Deciding ahead of time how to get help is a proactive and healthy way to encourage emotional health in your marriage. This vision also might require you to find safe couples with whom you can share real problems and feelings. Some of these people may become accountability partners for you—those who will help you follow through with your plans to make changes in your life.

I spent some time talking to Clara about her dating relationships after she was divorced. She was very concerned about making the same choices in another relationship. She came in one day and proudly told me she'd decided to ask her current boyfriend if he would be willing to go to counseling if they started having trouble. She told him she wouldn't marry anyone who wouldn't agree to get help if they struggled. Clara is a woman with a clear vision for emotional health!

Work

By *work*, I mean a task you and your husband share. While each of you might have your own career, you also need to have something you accomplish together. It could be income-producing or volunteer work, a home improvement project or a joint service commitment at church. You might start a small business or volunteer for a community charity, school committee, or nonprofit organization. Or you might find ways to support each other in your existing work. For example, Alan helped put together some marketing brochures for his wife's company because he had more computer expertise. Leslie helped organize the results of her husband's latest research project. Having a vision for the way you connect through work helps you feel included in each other's lives.

Lynn was an interior decorator, so she found it easy to take control of any decisions regarding the house. In the first years of marriage, Lynn independently made all of the choices concerning wall colors, furniture, and art in their home. Since Ben was often busy at his office, he didn't mind. But as they began to create a vision together, he showed interest in being involved in house decisions, so they began to spend their Saturdays shopping together for unique art and furniture. They not only enjoyed the outings they planned, but they also had stories that accompanied the art pieces they purchased. The space they shared at home became more and more *theirs*.

Social Life

How is your social life as a couple? You're not alone if you admit to not having many or any couple friends. Talking about what you desire as a couple is most important here. Some couples are fulfilled primarily by socializing with family. Others are starved for interaction with other couples but don't know how to go about establishing new relationships. Knowing what each of you wants is the first step toward making it happen.

When creating a vision for any of the five areas, you'll first want to discuss your life history in that area. In the case of your social life, you'll find it helpful to consider the following questions: Have you ever had good friendships with other couples? Did your parents model close friendships with other couples? Have you experienced hurtful relationships that make you more cautious about friendships today? Talking about these issues will help you understand each other better and also help you determine the roadblocks to creating a new vision and acting on it.

Danielle was very involved with her career friends, and she did most of her socializing without her husband. He was a doctor and had little time to think about a social life anyway, so he hadn't pushed her to seek friendships with other couples. But as they became companions through their healing process, their desires began to change. Both voiced a need to find a few couples they would enjoy spending time with. Their initial vision was to find two couples they could invite to dinner or an event. They agreed to socialize with one couple each month. Slowly they were able to make joint friendships that they both enjoyed, and they didn't put excessive pressure on their relationship to make the change.

Sexuality

Sexuality in your relationship is much more than just a decision about frequency. If you are learning how to be intimate emotionally and spiritually with each other, sexual intercourse shouldn't be the only way you feel close to each other. So often, sexual closeness is the barometer couples use to determine emotional closeness. If you are having good sex, you might think you are close and connected. However, true intimacy with your husband is accomplished by sharing feelings, needs, perceptions, core beliefs, and desires in a safe environment, knowing you won't be blamed, judged, or rejected if you do. Intimacy is about being loved unconditionally. And when you can connect in such a way, sexual sharing will be an expression of that bond.

How will you decide to create a healthy sexual vision? Talking about your sex life is just as important as talking about all of the other areas of your shared vision. You'll want to include information about what kinds of sexual activity you enjoy. What kinds of sexual touch? How often do you desire to be sexual? What kinds of things help you to be available to sexual sharing? Most couples feel very embarrassed about intentionally stating a desire to be sexual or talking about feelings before, during, or after sexual intercourse. You could have a conversation about the vulnerability you feel in this area. You might begin by discussing the messages you received about your sexuality when you were young—from your family, church, and culture. You might describe how you feel about initiating sexual touch or responding to it. You can learn a lot about each other by talking about the times when you feel rejected in your sex life and the ways you deal with such rejection. You might decide to be abstinent for a while for the purpose of growing closer to each other through other kinds of sharing. Finally, if you desire additional help to achieve healthy sexuality in your marriage, you might consider reading relevant books together or consulting a therapist who can help you work through deeper issues you might have.

Roberto and Rena struggled to enjoy each other sexually after participating in a recovery program for his sexual addiction for eighteen months. During their work, she began talking about her sexual abuse as a child for the first time and the triggers she was now able to identify for herself. He was worried that being sexual at all would ignite compulsive sexual thoughts, and he was tempted to refrain from any sexual contact to stay sober. After attaining emotional and spiritual intimacy through their hard work, they made a commitment to work with a sex therapist who could lead them through specific exercises to rejuvenate their sexual intimacy. With tools to help them state feelings honestly, set safe boundaries, ask for needs to be met, and practice empathy with each other, they were well on their way to creating a new sexual vision and a much more satisfying sex life.

Spiritual Life

Most of us would agree that our spiritual life as a couple is important, but we often tend to think about what we can do individually to grow in our faith rather than how we can create a vision together. Most churches have men's ministries and women's ministries, but couples' ministries are less common. You will find greater spiritual intimacy if you work at finding ways to share your spiritual life. If you believe God will use your pain for a purpose, then finding ways to share your pain or your talents together and serve others will bless your marriage.

As a couple, think about the adversities God has helped you endure. In what way can you take what you have learned and provide hope to someone else? Or take stock of your special gifts. What do you do well? Sing? Create plays? Provide hospitality? Offer lay counseling? Pray for couples together? Open your home for Bible studies? Teach children? There are countless ways you can be a team and honor God with your spiritual vision to serve him as a couple.

After working on their individual growth in therapy groups for two years, Sheila and Luke decided to offer a six-week series for couples at their church. They used some of the tools they'd learned to provide a user-friendly platform for couples wanting to talk about real issues in their marriage. As part of the series, Sheila and Luke shared their testimony of the struggles they had overcome.

Katrina and Paul were missionaries and lived on the mission field for years with the secrets of his sexual addiction. After they came back to the United States for their own healing, they returned with a greater vision for their spiritual life: they chose to be honest about their struggles and to lead others to a life of purity. They worked as a team, talking to men, women, and couples. And through their own pain, they grew deeper in their spiritual life together.

Henrietta and Karl decided to create a choir for young women. Besides believing in the girls and coaching them in confidence and truth about themselves, Henrietta and Karl planned to give the proceeds from concerts to worthy causes.

The possibilities to serve God as a couple are endless, but doing so will take intentional planning. Start with a short vision statement of how you see yourselves serving together, and go from there.

Prioritizing, Sacrificing, and Grieving Losses

As a couple, you may want to explore many other areas of vision: parenting, education, recreation, careers, physical health, and finances, to name a few. When you are creating a vision together, you'll be continually interweaving these dimensions, some overriding others when priorities shift. For instance, your desire to set aside a certain amount of money for recreation may be sacrificed for the purpose of spending resources to go on a mission trip (spiritual life). Or your vision to spend time with friends (social life) might be delayed for a time while you work on emotional healing. Or you may choose to reduce your income for a few years while you go back to school. When you are intentional about your shared vision, you can endure the losses that may result when one aspect of your vision supersedes another. Having a shared vision helps you know *what* you want to do as a couple. Being intentional helps you find passion and purpose in your choices.

I remember when Mark and I created our vision to work full time together in ministry. Our vision statement was "to teach, speak, write, and counsel for sexual integrity and wholeness." To pursue our new vision, I needed to leave my company, where I had worked for more than twenty years. We both felt led by God to pursue this new vision together, and I *chose* to leave my former work. But I also felt great loss at leaving something I truly loved. My emotions were confusing to me at first: How could I feel so sad when I *wanted* this new vision with my husband? I realized that with change, I could feel both—sadness and excitement. I needed considerable time to grieve the life I was leaving. The freedom to be sad with Mark and his patience and compassion while I worked through my sadness allowed us to be allies—to be connected intimately while working on our new vision.

In *Sacred Marriage*, Thomas writes, "What both of us crave more than anything else is to be intimately close to the God who made us. If that relationship is right, we won't make such severe demands on our marriage, asking each other, expecting each other, to compensate for spiritual emptiness."[3]

A New "I Do"

Who we become in our relationship is just as important as *what* we do together. If you come to your couple's vision with your life full of passion, worth, and companionship with the Lord, you will be able to put your needs and desires on hold at times while you serve your husband. You can become "Jesus with skin on" for each other—extending patience, grace, mercy, empathy, forgiveness, and compassion. That is the Christlike character I seek to make my own.

These were the words I wrote to Mark when we renewed our wedding vows seventeen years after we were married. My vision for our relationship had changed significantly from the vision I had when I spoke my first "I do" at age twenty-one.

Let me love you without possessing you ...
Let me share my feelings with you, knowing you will handle them with care but not responsibility ... Let me express my needs, knowing you can fulfill them only sometimes ... Let my need for aloneness at times be not a rejection of you, but a time of nourishment for me ... Let me not depend on your affirmations of me but live assuredly in the well-being of my own soul.

Let us be honest with each other ...
Knowing we won't be ridiculed or threatened or ignored ... Let us both find good friends without those friendships being a threat to the life we share ... Let us respond to each other without judgment or expectation, rejoicing in the moment

to share intimately ... Let us be weak sometimes or strong sometimes, knowing that both contribute to the growth of our relationship.

Let us dream together ...
With the playfulness of a child ... Let our love be a wellspring for the renewal of our own "little children," the safe place to nurture all of our feelings, the playground to experience God's abundant life.

Let us begin again today!

Thinking It Over

1. Have you lost parts of yourself as you have sought to serve your husband and family? What have you sacrificed that you desire to reclaim? Or what do you desire to do or be that you have yet to begin?

2. What stage are you currently in as you develop your relationship — enmeshment, differentiation, practicing, reengagement, or mutual interdependence? What do you need to work on to be able to move to the next stage?

3. Which dimensions of vision: emotional health, work, social life, sexuality, or spiritual life, do you like to work on the most? Which are the hardest to think about and talk about?

4. What are some of your roadblocks to creating a vision for yourself or with your husband?

5. What does a "passionate alliance" look like to you? How can you be more intentional about creating a shared vision?

Taking Your Show
on the Road

I don't want to be in therapy my whole life," wailed a woman in group recently. I don't want you to be either! The purpose of entering a healing journey with the help of others is to equip yourself to "take your show on the road." As I practiced long hours with a coach and teammates to be a better tennis player, my real desire was to get into matches so I could try out what I had learned. You, too, have been learning how to be "match ready," and your matches are waiting for you everywhere you go.

Eventually your healing will lead you to practice your new relating skills with everyone you know—your kids, your colleagues, your friends and family, your husband, and God. How will you do in your relationships when you get out of your "safe" environment? Will you risk being vulnerable? How will you practice being authentic? What will you do when you are stressed, angered, or stretched beyond your capabilities? What will you do if you are hurt again? With whom will you choose to be honest? Will you remember to have accountability in your life, or will you go back to trying to manage everything alone? Will you take care of yourself? Do you know how important it is to surrender your control? Whom will you trust? Taking your show on the road will require you to have healthy answers to these questions.

Taking your show on the road doesn't mean that you'll no longer struggle, that all of your relationships will be fabulous, or that you'll never have unwanted feelings. But you will know your triggers, your needs, your options, and the lessons you can learn from each situation. In the past, figuring out some of these stuck places may have taken you months. Now you may be able to get out of a coping place and choose healthy behaviors in only days or hours or minutes. That's a sign of emotional and spiritual growth. God uses our whole life to grow our character. He doesn't waste one crisis or one relationship. When you are ready to be a lifelong student of his, you will be marching down a road with endless possibilities to grow.

When you take your show on the road, you'll need to be able to find safe people along the way—not just your support group or your therapist or pastor. Having safe people allows you to talk about the real issues in your life so you don't live with unfinished business festering inside and silently killing you. You'll need to keep current with your feelings and not let emotions build up or blow up. You will feel more peaceful and genuine when your insides match your outsides. Road trips require oil changes and tire pressure checks, so you should be mindful of when you need a tune-up with a professional to check out your emotional health.

When you are "on the road" after your own journey, you'll look for the stories behind the people you meet. Now that you have been trained to look deeper, you can look for meaning in the behaviors of people—all of the possibilities of pain and wounded-ness that drive people to do what they do. You will continue to let go of your old black-and-white thinking and the temptation to fix people. You will remember that there is no one right way or one right explanation for anything.

Did I fill the world with love my whole life through? A homemade wooden plaque with this verse hung in our home when we first married. It was a vision for our new life together. I had no idea I would learn to love differently through sexual betrayal. I have new eyes to see the world. Whereas I used to focus on *what* people were doing, I now focus on *why* they might be doing what they're doing. The stories behind the lives I see are worthy. Every time I'm privileged to know someone's story, my capacity to love enlarges.

Nothing about your betrayal and your subsequent work to understand and grow has been a waste. I hear such complaints regularly: "If only I had known about his sexual struggles before I married him. Now I've wasted my life." No matter how many years you lived with a lie, no matter what the lie was, no matter how long it took to get help, it is worth every day if you've found a new life, whether together or apart. God's timing is what it is for a good reason. We don't usually understand the why or when of our exposure to betrayal. But looking back, would you ever have signed up for such a journey of self-discovery? Would you ever have known the meaning of surrender and dependence on God if he hadn't allowed this tragedy to enter your life?

Giving back to others out of your wisdom and experience is a way of grounding your growth. I marvel at the way Mark can read or listen to great ideas and remember them so clearly in speeches or therapy sessions. When I told him I admired this quality, he simply said, "If you teach what you've heard like I do, you're much more likely to remember it." Grounding your newfound knowledge of growth is no different. We hammer home the truths we've learned and practiced by sharing with others.

Your road has taken you through a lot of pain. In *The Purpose Driven Life*, Rick Warren reminds us, "Our greatest lessons come out of pain.... Problems force you to focus on God, draw you closer to others in fellowship, build Christlike character, provide you with a ministry, and give you a testimony. Every problem is purpose-driven."[1]

God is ready to use your pain. You have been hurt, but my hope is that through this book, you have sought to understand the greater purpose behind your suffering. Your husband's betrayal was about the pain in his life; your reaction was about the pain in yours. You have taken time to feel how betrayal has affected you. You know the importance of grieving your losses. You have been asked to accept that God had lessons for you to learn in your pain and that there is meaning in the suffering you have endured. You have grown and know that in all circumstances you have choices; you don't need to be a victim bound by anger or bitterness. You have practiced being authentic—knowing your feelings and stating them, expressing your needs, owning what you need to change to become the woman God calls you to be. You are softer, more approachable, more serene, more accepting, more surrendered to God. The fruit of the Spirit is your reward for the hard work of examining your life: love, joy, peace, patience, kindness, goodness, faithfulness, gentleness, and self-control (Gal. 5:22).

Sometimes you don't even realize how much you have grown until you start looking back or sharing what you've learned with others. Two women who had started a group together a year ago met again recently. Tina had left group after a few weeks, but when she met Diane, who had been working on her issues for over a year, she was astounded at the change she saw. "How did you do it?" Tina asked.

Diane was taken aback, not realizing she was so different. "After struggling to control Scott's use of the computer and attempting to be a detective so he would never be able to hide anything from me again, I finally decided to look at my own flaws. After I made a list of all of the things I didn't like about myself, I started to make changes. I decided I didn't care who liked me or not—I was going to like myself! I started with my body, then my anger, then my fear of loneliness, then my need to be needed." Diane was describing the process of healing from sexual betrayal. She was becoming a new woman.

My life would have been very different if I hadn't been thrown onto a road less traveled when adversity hit. It would have been filled with superficial relationships centered around trivial interests—"How are the kids?" "Where did you vacation?" "What is your new house like?" "Where do you work?" But the tragedy of sexual betrayal gave me a new arena of connection: the pain of humanity. It is from this place that I most deeply experience God in my life as he loves me through my pain and lets me serve others in theirs. George Eliot wrote a favorite verse of mine years ago: "What do we live for if not to make life less difficult for each other?"

The great wisdom in the full version of Reinhold Neibuhr's "Serenity Prayer" reminds me of the big picture.

> *God, grant me the serenity*
> *To accept the things I cannot change,*
> *Courage to change the things I can,*
> *And wisdom to know the difference.*
> *Living one day at a time;*
> *Enjoying one moment at a time;*
> *Accepting hardship as the pathway to peace;*
> *Taking, as Jesus did, this sinful world as it is,*
> *Not as I would have it;*
> *Trusting that He will make all things right*
> *If I surrender to His will;*
> *That I may be reasonably happy in this life*
> *And supremely happy with Him forever in the next.*
> *Amen.*

Long ago I worried that I would be defined by sexual betrayal for the rest on my life. Today I am defined by character traits that developed out of my journey through pain. Only God is big enough to show me triumph over tragedy.

I pray that reading this book has helped you know yourself and your story more completely. Before you began this journey toward healing from sexual betrayal, you only knew what you knew! Now you have acquainted yourself with the stories of other women walking through their pain, and when you know stories, you gain new perceptions, more patience, greater empathy, and an ability to love with less judgment and criticism. You are on the road to showing the world something about unconditional love. It is a "show" that will honor God and continue to heal your heart.

Depression Assessment

When you become aware of sexual betrayal in your marriage, you will face many overwhelming feelings: anger, sadness, anxiety, confusion, and hopelessness, to name a few. In the months that follow, it will be important to acquire the help you need to process your feelings and to manage your life. Sometimes it is enough to talk to other safe women. Finding a therapist or pastor to talk to will be helpful to others. And sometimes it may be necessary to have medical help to relieve feelings that have become unmanageable.

The following identifying symptoms are listed in *Unveiling Depression in Women.*[1] It is important to remember that when assessing depression, you will want to have a complete physical exam to rule out any other physical conditions you may have, as well as a complete evaluation by a psychologist, psychiatrist, or medical doctor who is qualified to assess your symptoms in the context of your life's experiences.

Here is the list they provided:

Mood/Emotions

☐ Depressed mood: feelings of helplessness, worthlessness, sadness, irritability, and pessimism for most of the day

☐ Excessive crying or an inability to cry or express emotion

☐ Feelings of worthlessness, hopelessness, inappropriate guilt, or blaming yourself for your problems

☐ Loss of interest in previously pleasurable activities; inability to enjoy usual hobbies or activities, including sex

☐ Unresolved grief issues

Thoughts

☐ Inability to concentrate, remember things, make decisions, or think clearly, even on routine tasks

☐ Obsessing over negative experiences or thoughts

☐ Low self-esteem

☐ Recurrent thoughts of suicide or death; you may have already made a will and begun thinking about your funeral

☐ Feeling pessimistic about your life

☐ Attitude of, "What difference does it make?"

Physical Functioning

☐ Appetite disturbance, eating far less or far more than usual

☐ Sleep disturbances: inability to sleep, tossing and turning, not being able to get back to sleep, sleeping too much, or irregular sleep patterns

☐ Constant fatigue or loss of energy

☐ Slow, soft speech

☐ Chronic aches and pains that don't respond to treatment

☐ Anxiety or panic attacks

☐ Unexplained headaches, backaches, abdominal pain, constipation, or general aches and pains

Spiritual Factors

☐ Feeling that God is very distant

☐ Being angry and disappointed in God

☐ Having no hope for your future

☐ Feeling abandoned and forsaken by God

☐ Feeling a heaviness in your spirit

☐ Feeling like a cloud of darkness is over you

Behavior Factors

☐ Observable restlessness, irritability, or decreased activity

☐ Substance abuse such as alcohol or drugs

☐ Suicide attempts

☐ Decreased performance at work or school

☐ Social withdrawal: refusal to go out, to see friends, and avoidance of old friends

☐ Avoidance of situations that could cause responsibility or failure

☐ Dislike of crowds

☐ Difficulty getting along with others

As Hart and Weber summarize, this is a list of symptoms that can alert you to the possibility of depression. The more symptoms you can identify, the more possible is depression.

I experienced many of these symptoms after receiving the unexpected and shocking information of sexual betrayal. It is the job for each of us to know how we will define and receive treatment for our symptoms. There is no "one right answer."

For further reference, Hart and Weber list numerous websites and books in the resource section of their book.

Resources

Resources that provide help for sexual purity issues are changing daily. With the Internet, it is possible to search general topics and find many resources. Rather than endorse or refer you to specific therapists, organizations, or ministries, I would encourage you to research the resources available to find the right "fit."

I found that by submersing myself in books about recovery, I could eventually begin trusting what I needed and wanted. There are many people and books that address sexual betrayal and personal growth. The theories and suggestions vary as much as night and day. By educating yourself, you will begin to know what feels *right* for you! Listen to the wisdom that God has given you, and follow that lead.

Twelve-step groups and support groups are very helpful in connecting peers who are committed to change and grow. Many of these require only a nominal fee or are free to attend. The quality of support groups varies from group to group and city to city. If you have vision for what you want in your life, you will want to surround yourself with people who support your vision.

Websites

www.celebraterecovery.com
> Celebrate Recovery is a faith-based program to help those struggling with hurts, habits, and hang-ups by showing them the loving power of Jesus Christ through a recovery process. This program is not specific to sexual betrayal.

www.coda.org
> Co-Dependents Anonymous is a 12-step fellowship of men and women whose common purpose is to develop healthy relationships.

Patterns and characteristics of codependency are offered as a tool to aid participants in self-evaluation.

www.cosa-recovery.org

Codependents of Sexual Addiction Anonymous is a 12-step recovery program for men and women whose lives have been affected by another person's compulsive sexual behavior: "... a program for spiritual development, no matter what your religious beliefs."

www.faithfulandtrueministries.com

Faithful & True Ministries is the Minneapolis-based ministry of Mark and Debra Laaser. This website will provide resources, articles about addiction, and information about counseling, training, and workshops available at their counseling center.

www.freedomeveryday.org

L.I.F.E. Ministries (Living in Freedom Everyday) is a Florida-based ministry that provides support materials for people working on sexual purity issues in their lives. Their site lists groups around the country that use their L.I.F.E. Guides.

www.overcomersoutreach.org

Overcomers Outreach is a bridge between the traditional 12-step programs and the church. Through applying the truth of Scripture, working the 12-steps, and sharing in fellowship with other overcomers, OO participants let go of past hurts, triumph over current problems, and learn to depend on God.

www.sanon.org

S-Anon International is a 12-step group for persons who have a friend or family member with a sexual addiction.

www.webmd.com/sex/Sex-Love-Addiction

WebMD is an expansive website that lists explanations, treatment, and referrals for many physical ailments. This specific link contains many of the secular websites for support groups and lists contact information and general statistics about the organizations.

Books

This list includes some of the books that have been meaningful to me in my recovery. They are written by both secular and Christian authors. I am constantly adding "favorites" to my list as I receive recommendations from others in the process of finding authentic recovery.

Sexual Addiction

Breaking Free: Understanding Sexual Addiction and the Healing Power of Jesus, Russell Willingham and Bob Davies (Downers Grove: InterVarsity, 1999).

Don't Call It Love, Patrick Carnes (New York: Bantam, 1991).

Faithful and True Workbook, Mark Laaser (Nashville, Tenn.: Lifeway, 1996).

Healing the Wounds of Sexual Addiction, Mark Laaser (Grand Rapids: Zondervan, 1992). Formerly titled *Faithful & True.*

In the Shadows of the Net, Patrick Carnes, David Delmonico, and Elizabeth Griffin (Center City, Minn.: Hazelden, 2001).

Is It Love or Is It Addiction?, Brenda Schaeffer (Center City, Minn.: Hazelden, 1997).

A L.I.F.E. Guide: Men Living in Freedom Everyday, Mark Laaser (Fairfax, Va.: Xulon, 2002).

Out of the Shadows, Patrick Carnes (Minneapolis, Minn.: CompCare Publishers, 1992).

Pornography Trap, Ralph Earle & Mark Laaser (Kansas City, Kans.: Beacon Hill, 2002).

Coaddiction/Codependency

Back From Betrayal, Jennifer Schneider (Tucson: Recovery Resources Press, 2001).

Beyond Codependency, Melody Beattie (New York: Harper/Hazelden, 1989).

Boundaries and Relationships, Charles L. Whitfield (Deerfield Beach, Fla.: Health Communications, 1993).

Codependent No More, Melody Beattie (New York: Harper/Hazelden, 1987).

Codependents' Guide to the Twelve Steps, Melody Beattie (New York: Simon & Schuster, 1990).

Facing Codependence, Pia Mellody (New York: Harper/SanFrancisco, 1989).

A L.I.F.E. Guide: Spouses Living in Freedom Everyday, Melissa Haas (Grand Rapids: Color House Graphics, 2005).

Lost in the Shuffle, Robert Subby (Deerfield Beach, Fla.: Health Communication, Inc., 1987).

Love Is a Choice, Robert Hemfelt, Frank Minirth, and Paul Meier (Nashville: Thomas Nelson, 1989).

Sexual and Emotional Abuse

Courage to Heal, Ellen Bass and Laura Davis (New York: Harper & Row, 1988).

Emotional Incest Syndrome, Patricia Love (New York: Bantam, 1990).

Silently Seduced: Understanding Covert Incest, Kenneth M. Adams (Deerfield Beach, Fla.: Health Communications, 1991).

On the Threshold of Hope, Diane Langberg (Wheaton: Tyndale, 1999).

The Wounded Heart, Dan B. Allender (Colorado Springs: Navpress, 1990).

Family of Origin/Looking at Your Past

Adult Children: The Secrets of Dysfunctional Families, John Friel and Linda Friel (Deerfield Beach, Fla.: Health Communications, 1988).

An Adult Child's Guide to What's Normal, John Friel and Linda Friel, Deerfield Beach, Fla.: Health Communications, Inc., 1990).

The Blessing, Gary Smalley and John Trent (Nashville: Thomas Nelson, 1986).

The Betrayal Bond, Patrick Carnes (Deerfield Beach, Fla.: Health Communications, 1997).

Healing the Child Within, Charles Whitfield (Deerfield Beach, Fla.: Health Communications, 1987).

Healing the Shame That Binds You, John Bradshaw (Deerfield Beach, Fla.: Health Communications, 1988).

Homecoming, John Bradshaw (New York: Bantam, 1990).

Released from Shame: Recovery for Adult Children of Dysfunctional Families, Sandra Wilson (Downers Grove: InterVarsity, 1990).

Sexuality

The Celebration of Sex, Doug Rosenau (Nashville: Thomas Nelson, 1994).

Restoring the Pleasure, Cliff Penner & Joyce Penner (Dallas: Word, 1993).

Secrets of Eve, Archibald Hart, Catherine Hart Weber, and Debra Taylor (Nashville: Word, 1998).

Sexual Anorexia, Patrick Carnes (Center City, Minn.: Hazelden, 1997).

Sexual Healing Journey, Wendy Maltz (New York: Harper Perennial, 1992).

Talking to Your Kids About Sex, Mark Laaser (Colorado Springs: WaterBrook, 1999).

Couples Recovery

Before a Bad Goodbye, Tim Clinton (Nashville: Word, 1999).

Fit to Be Tied, Bill and Lynne Hybels (Grand Rapids: Zondervan, 1991).

Getting the Love You Want, Harville Hendrix (New York: Henry Holt and Company, 1988).

Open Hearts: Renewing Relationships with Recovery, Romance & Reality, Patrick Carnes, Debra Laaser, and Mark Laaser (Wickenburg, Ariz.: Gentle Path Press, 1999).

In Quest of the Mythical Mate, Ellyn Bader and Peter Pearson (New York: Brunner/Mazel, Inc., 1988).

Sacred Marriage, Gary Thomas (Grand Rapids: Zondervan, 2000).

Torn Asunder: Recovering from Extramarital Affairs, Dave Carder (Chicago: Moody Press, 1991).

General Recovery/Well-Being

Addiction and Grace, Gerald May (New York: Harper, 1988).

Adrenaline and Stress, Archibald Hart (Nashville: W Publishing Group, 1995).

The Anxiety Cure, Archibald Hart (Nashville: W Publishing Group, 1999).

Boundaries, Henry Cloud & John Townsend (Grand Rapids: Zondervan, 1992).

The Dance of Anger, Harriet Lerner (New York: HarperCollins, 1985).

The Dance of Connection, Harriet Lerner (New York: HarperCollins, 2001).

The Dance of Intimacy, Harriet Lerner (New York: HarperCollins, 1990).

Gentle Path through the Twelve Steps, Patrick Carnes (Center City, Minn.: Hazelden, 1993).

How People Grow, Henry Cloud & John Townsend (Grand Rapids: Zondervan, 2001).

Love Is a Choice, Robert Hemfelt, Frank Minirth and Paul Meier (Nashville: Thomas Nelson, 1989).

Margin: Restoring Emotional, Physical, Financial and Time Reserves to Overloaded Lives, Richard Swenson (Colorado Springs: NavPress, 2004).

Safe People, Henry Cloud & John Townsend (Grand Rapids: Zondervan, 1995).

Unveiling Depression in Women, Archibald Hart and Catherine Hart (Grand Rapids: Revell, 2002).

Inspirational

Into Abba's Arms: Finding the Acceptance You've Always Wanted, Sandra D. Wilson (Wheaton: Tyndale, 1998).

The Dream Giver, Bruce Wilkinson (Sisters, Ore.: Multnomah, 2003).

Everybody's Normal Till You Get to Know Them, John Ortberg (Grand Rapids: Zondervan, 2003).

If You Want to Walk on Water, You've Got to Get Out of the Boat, John Ortberg, (Grand Rapids: Zondervan, 2001).

The Inner Voice of Love: A Journey through Anguish to Freedom, Henri Nouwen (New York: Image Books, 1996).

The Journey of Recovery: A New Testament (Colorado Springs: International Bible Society, 2006).

The Purpose Driven Life, Rick Warren (Grand Rapids: Zondervan, 2002).

The Return of the Prodigal Son, Henri Nouwen (New York: Image Books, 1994).

Shattered Dreams: God's Unexpected Pathway to Joy, Larry Crabb (Colorado Springs: WaterBrook, 2001).

Total Forgiveness, R. T. Kendall (Lake Mary, Fla.: Charisma House,
2002).

When the Heart Waits, Sue Monk Kidd, (New York: HarperCollins,
1990).

Meditation

*Answers in the Heart: Daily Meditations for Men and Women Recovering from
Sex Addiction* (San Francisco: Harper/Hazelden, 1989).

Each Day a New Beginning: Daily Meditations for Women (San Francisco:
Harper/Hazelden, 1982).

Meditations for Women Who Do Too Much, Anne Wilson Schaef (New
York: HarperCollins, 1990).

Serenity: A Companion for Twelve Step Recovery, Drs. Hemfelt and Fowler
(Nashville: Thomas Nelson, 1990).

Notes

Chapter 1:
What Am I Supposed to Do Now?

1. Jon Kabat-Zinn, *Wherever You Go, There You Are* (New York: Hyperion, 1994), xiii.
2. Drs. Henry Cloud and John Townsend, *Boundaries in Marriage* (Grand Rapids: Zondervan, 1999), 20.

Chapter 2:
Why Should I Get Help When It's His Problem?

1. John Ortberg, *Everybody's Normal Till You Get to Know Them* (Grand Rapids: Zondervan, 2003), 15.
2. Ibid., 18.
3. Melissa Haas, *A L.I.F.E. Guide: Spouses Living in Freedom Everyday* (Lake Mary, Fla.: L.I.F.E. Ministries International, 2005). You can order the guide at www.freedomeveryday.org.
4. I first heard this terminology on an audio tape of a speech given by John Ortberg entitled "Living the Life You Want" (conference of the American Association of Christian Counselors, Nashville).

Chapter 3:
How Could This Have Happened?

1. Mark describes his story and these dynamics of hundreds of men in his books and speeches. For example, see his first book, *Healing the Wounds of Sexual Addiction* (Grand Rapids: Zondervan, 2004).
2. John Banmen, ed., *Applications of the Satir Growth Model* (Sea Tac, Wash.: Avanta, The Virginia Satir Network, 2006), 13.
3. Our book *The Seven Desires of Every Heart* (Zondervan, 2008) will discuss more completely the iceberg model and the desires of the heart.
4. Gary Thomas, *Sacred Marriage* (Grand Rapids: Zondervan, 2002), 25–6.

Chapter 4:
Where Can I Hide My Heart?

1. Drs. Henry Cloud and John Townsend, *How People Grow* (Grand Rapids: Zondervan, 2001), 227–8.
2. Definition by Mark Laaser as used in speaking and teaching.
3. Archibald Hart and Catherine Hart Weber, *Unveiling Depression in Women: A Practical Guide to Understanding and Overcoming Depression* (Grand Rapids: Revell, 2002), 68, 41.
4. Cloud and Townsed, *How People Grow*, 234.

5. Judith Viorst, *Necessary Losses: The Loves, Illusions, Dependencies, and Impossible Expecta-tions That All of Us Have to Give Up in Order to Grow* (New York: Ballantine, 1986), 3.

6. Larry Crabb, *Shattered Dreams: God's Unexpected Pathway to Joy* (Colorado Springs: WaterBrook, 2001), 35.

Chapter 5:
When Will I Stop Feeling So Out of Control?

1. *Twelve Steps and Twelve Traditions* (New York: Alcoholics Anonymous World Services, 1952), 73.

2. Ibid., 75.

3. Rick Warren, *The Purpose Driven Life* (Grand Rapids: Zondervan, 2002), 274–5.

Chapter 6:
What Do You Mean, "Do I Want to Get Well"?

1. Warren, *Purpose Driven Life*, 193, 197, 199.

2. Emilie Barnes with Anne Christian Buchanan, *A Journey through Cancer* (Eugene, Ore.: Harvest House, 2003), 104.

3. Ibid., 100.

Chapter 8:
Is Forgiving Him Really Possible?

1. The principles of forgiveness included in this chapter have been adapted from R. T. Kendall, *Total Forgiveness* (Lake Mary, Fla.: Charisma House, 2002), 1–35. Used by permission.

2. R. T. Kendall, *Total Forgiveness* (Lake Mary, Fla.: Charisma House, 2002), 86. Used by permission.

Chapter 9:
How Can We Rebuild Our Relationship?

1. Ellyn Bader, PhD, and Peter Pearson, PhD, *In Quest of the Mythical Mate: A Developmen-tal Approach to Diagnosis and Treatment in Couples Therapy* (New York: Brunner/Mazel, 1998). Used by permission.

2. Gary Thomas, *Sacred Marriage* (Grand Rapids: Zondervan, 2002), 23 (italics in original).

3. Ibid., 24.

Epilogue

1. Rick Warren, *The Purpose Driven Life* (Grand Rapids: Zondervan, 2002), 309.

Depression Assessment

1. Archibald Hart, PhD and Catherine Hart Weber, PhD, *Unveiling Depression in Women* (Grand Rapids: Revell, 2002), 37.